CROWNED HARP

CROWNED HARP

Memories of the Last Years of the Crown
in Ireland

By

NORA ROBERTSON

Illustrations by Ian Gray

1960
ALLEN FIGGIS & CO. LTD.,
DUBLIN.

MADE AND PRINTED IN THE
REPUBLIC OF IRELAND BY
O'GORMAN LTD., GALWAY.

CONTENTS

Dedicated by a Septuagenarian to her Grandchildren.

FOREWORD.

The average Englishman spending a holiday in Ireland rather enjoys not understanding the agreeable natives. It makes him feel both perceptive and normal. If he decides to prolong his visit, even by 300 years, he will at the end find himself nearly — but not quite — the same. Although he has not become wholly Irish neither is he, as he used to be, wholly English. He has become that hybrid, mercifully not a sterile one, an Anglo-Irishman and can remain such for hundreds of years. Anglo-Irish merely means an Englishman resident in Ireland, not like Anglo-Indian which implies mixed blood and colour. The hyphen forming the compound word should be the connecting link drawing the ends together ; unfortunately it sometimes pushes them apart as ethnic incompatibles. We Anglo-Irish residents in Ireland are certainly not passengers ; we have acquired many deeply personal relations and these involve duty and service to the State " to which it has pleased God to call Protestants ". For Protestants we most of us are. The religious gulf between us and the Roman Catholic majority is properly regarded as an individual matter and certainly in the South no minority could be treated more graciously than we are. But, because we feel respect for Irish flag and anthem, we are surely not expected to abandon our traditional affection for the loyalties of our youth ? Our grandchildren must make their own adjustments in their own time, but we who were reared under the Crowned Harp cannot be asked to desert the Crown now that we honour the Harp first.

This resistance to becoming wholly Irish is often resented, yet Irishmen in the United States or Australia preserve their national identity without disloyalty to the countries of their adoption. " Mother " nations appear to hold their sons more tenaciously than do those that are newly evolved. Dual loyalty is not necessarily disruptive and need not cause confusion. Since our Anglo-Irish Protestant elements comprise only 5% of the population, our attitude may appear unimportant, yet the confiscations of history have given us so much the best of the material bargain that we still retain one third of the country's wealth and influence. It is surely magnanimous that this inequality is not more resented and that the young Government which took over after the Treaty should have volunteered generous concessions to encourage our members to stay on. We were thought to possess character and experience that should be useful to the new State. Let us hope that after 40 years we have earned our salt, certainly as neighbours, if less conspicuously in political life and while remaining somewhat aloof from the official Harp. Why aloof ? Perhaps it is because we still feel Anglo-Irish and not Gaelic, in which latter we have no race tradition ; we are also Protestant. We are unlike the first invaders from England who were neither English nor Protestant. They intermixed and intermarried freely with the Irish. Gaelic chieftains often served the Crown while Norman notables led rebellions for the Harp. Conflicts were for personal rather than for national ambition. The Reformation did not change the religion of Ireland but it established the English as a settlement on a long lease. I regret having to use the term Protestant so much but here it has become an unavoidable label, understood by all.

At a period of intense self-determination the adjustment of a small, prosperous minority of their own kin should be of interest to the original Home Country and therefore, as a septuagenarian, I presume to think that the transition is worth recounting. I am perhaps exceptionally well placed to reanimate the climate of those days, obscured through the complications of two World Wars. I belong to a family that has lived in Ireland for 350 years, Anglo-Irish indeed ; I spent most of my childhood in British barracks in Southern Ireland ; my father raised the XVIth Irish Division in close touch with John Redmond ; I sat next the King's representative at my father's funeral when we followed the Union Jack, and twenty years later I thanked the representative of Mr. de Valera for attending my husband's burial.

In 1925 we had returned from London to live in the Free State and my husband had co-operated with the appropriate department in the Town Planning of Dublin and Cork. In respecting new loyalties it had not seemed incumbent on us to throw our old ones overboard. I do not presume to attempt a formal *précis* of those years but only to record personal memories reflecting on the transfer.

CHAPTER I

FOREBEARS.

Those of us directly descended from the founders of the Elizabethan settlement feel a special kinship with them which is missing in the descendants of the Cromwellians. They were not mere grabbers, they were men of many parts, colonists in the fullest sense. Their wholesale excesses made them detested by those whom they conquered, but how much of this policy was due to inseparable characteristics of their age ? How much more considerate were the Irish Chiefs whom they defeated ? Their constructive qualities deserve to be better understood and in fairness to them the writings which they have left behind should be studied and accepted as part of their contradictory age.

Not the least of the heritage they have bequeathed to the Irish is the shape of the English language at its most expressive and dexterous. The use Irish writers have since made of it is one of the country's international glories. In Ireland, however, more criticism is expressed at the suppression of the Irish language.

My father, Lawrence Parsons, came of a cadet branch of a family that derived directly from the Elizabethan Munster Settlement. This particular generation of English adventurers opened the Indies and Americas and formed the most influential of the English settlements here where, if they did not actually introduce the Reformation, they worked to establish it and founded Trinity College, Dublin. They came firstly in quest of timber, a growing necessity for ships and houses, and were

11

soon involved in the conflicts between the Geraldines and the Desmond invaders from the North. Taking advantage of the local disarray they seized the wooded Blackwater district and its timber. First of these colonists almost to own Youghal and to become Mayor was Sir Walter Raleigh who was succeeded by my ancestor Lawrence Parsons at the delightful Tudor House of Myrtle Grove which still exists. It was there that the first long pipe was popularly supposed to have been smoked and from here voyages to the Indies were organised. Raleigh alluded to Parsons as " my comrade " but it was Parsons' kinsman, Richard Boyle, afterwards the great Earl of Cork, who mirrors Elizabethan personality most vividly. Boyle was the archetype of self-made man, efficient, predatory, dishonest and benevolent. His writings show a disingenuous self revelation that would enchant a psychologist. In Munster the vast districts he managed prospered unlike any others ; Youghal and Lismore blossomed under his *aegis*, but where he benefited he also robbed, especially his Church to which he imagined he was devoted.

He describes his arrival in Dublin in 1588, " all my wealth was twenty-seven pounds three shillings in money . . . . a taffeta doublett, cut with and upon taffeta, a pair of black velvet britches laced . . . . competent linnen and necessaries, with my rapier and dagger." Not a promising start for one who was to become the richest and most powerful man in Ireland. He battened as army contractor, owner of coal and iron mines and exchange banker. He ran a flourishing private business in London as money lender, posing as an Italian, "Mr. Burlamacchi," under which alias in later years he lent cash for speedy repayment to his pressed but beloved Monarch, King Charles.

Success in the Desmond Wars was followed by his adroit purchase of Raleigh's vacated estates. Thus, from around Youghal he came to dominate the scene. He was responsible for public works, schools and alms houses. He spent lavishly on himself and his large family and so behaved as the Irish like a paternal potentate to behave. Nationalists may deplore him ; the Irish people still have a friendly smile for his name. It is not surprising to learn that his kinsman Parsons did not have to stay long at Youghal. With the further connivance of his even less admirable brother, Lord Justice William Parsons, Lawrence acquired the forfeited estates of the Ely O'Carrolls in Offaly, whither he moved and erected Birr Castle ; here he and his established themselves and here the head of our family still lives.

It was in the spirit of his brothers-in-arms that Lord Cork's energy included expression by the pen. His " True Remembrances " and many attractive letters have not only personal but much public interest and all reveal breath-taking contradictions in an age of contradiction. It was part of these amazing men that they took a keen interest in natural history. Cork presented another of my ancestors, St. Ledger, with some young tench and carp which he had laboriously brought over from England to introduce into Munster.

His celebrated will dated 1642 is a heavily embroidered history of its time. William Parsons was left principal trustee. The various items named illuminate the period and show the range of interest and petty property on which he kept an active finger. Every relative has a special provision, every friend is mentioned. The crafty Lord Esmonde, who built the house where I am writing this, was co-trustee with Parsons and an *Item* provides him with " my best foot cloathe and furniture thereunto

belonging." *Item* " To my noble friend and cousin, the
Lord Justice Parsons, my sedan, lined with red wrought
velvet, . . . and brace of ducks every Summer during his
life . . . . " Sedan was probably the cloth, perhaps cloak
made in Sedan, as the more familiar chairs were then
barely known. Lawrence, a much greater friend, un-
luckily predeceased him or would no doubt have scored
some attractive *Item*.

Cork's monument in St. Mary's Church Youghal rivals
the Ormonde shrine at Kilkenny. He lies superb in effigy,
with a wife at head and heel ; his favourite mother-in-law
is commemorated at the top of the canopy ; his many
children are clustered like puppies around his magnif-
icently arrayed person. One of these children was later
to be honourably known to a wider world as Robert Boyle,
the scientist and co-founder of the Royal Society. Truly
there were brains besides brawn and boost behind that
special company of Adventurers.

Whilst the Muster wars have unending fascination for
historians their toll of misery was intense. What one has
learnt to call " guerilla " warfare and " genocide " led
to " scorched earth " and for a generation blood and
starvation cried out to God. The Irish chieftains invoked
Spanish aid and thus religion became interlocked with
nationality. In the after light of the Armada Victory
we are inclined to forget the frightening power of Spain.
Elizabethan soldiers bitterly begrudged the strain on
purse and arms which this Irish business entailed. We
have surely learnt by now how easily an appropriation
becomes the obvious harvest of the strong. The Irish
Desmond's own Palatinate had not fallen into their lap
as manna from Heaven ; it had been grabbed by the
mighty from the less mighty, at the expense of the still
more helpless and obscure. Admitting this it would still

be difficult, if not impossible, to-day to present the Elizabethan argument in such a way as to be excusable to an Irish descendant of those who were victimised by the policy. The situation was basically unnatural and unworkable. Neither full collaboration between the two peoples nor complete settlement by Englishmen was a feasible project.

We who are descended from these particular Elizabethans and largely owe our present status in this country to their activities are bound to feel somewhat identified with the personal struggle to solve the insoluble. Despite the horrors, it comprised so much that was admirable and of which we are still proud. We share their Faith and their sense of law ; their burning patriotism has been handed down to us. They considered themselves the Chosen People pledged to their Queen to destroy what was false or inconvenient.

To appreciate their view-point at the time no one is more revealing than Edmund Spencer who has been identified with some cruel acts and bitter comments ; yet it was he who wrote of the stragglers from the battles. "They were brought to such wretchedness that any stoney heart would rue the same. Out of every corner of the woods and glens they came, creeping upon their hands, for their legs would not bear them. They looked like Anatomies of death. They spoke like ghosts crying out of their graves." Spencer, whose young son had been burnt in his bed, had clearly kept his compassion. It is also interesting to learn that he did not suggest that the Irish were a peculiar lower race — they were merely underdeveloped. He sees them as objects for reform and realised that some of their leaders were educated men and excellent generals.

The pitiful consequences of chronic conflict upon standards of living aroused all his ardour for reform. He longed to improve the rough husbandry and roads and he foresaw forest clearings and protection from wolves. Above all he irked to discipline the barbarian for his own good.

It is an unfortunate fact that when a better-to-do nation compares itself with a much poorer one the actual poverty is confused with innate savagery. This happens even within the same nation. To French aristocrats the peasants appeared *canaille*. How natural for the prosperous English, conscious of their recently acquired civilised ways, to be appalled by the appearance and behaviour of the " Wilde " Irish. Not only did they speak a foolish foreign language, but they wore what any reasonable person must consider to be absurd clothes, and a preposterous hair cut (or non-cut). Moreover, they were much dirtier even than the English of that date. Imagine ourselves, even one of our kindest intellectuals, confronting a hairy creature, draped, as sole garment, in a single-piece coarse mantle ; his front hair (glibbe) falling over his face like a mask, his beard untouched, while ours was neat spade or torpedo, his huge foul hands outstretched to seize any weapon that would serve to flatten or to pierce us. Should we piously uplift our eyes and declare that we are all equal in the sight of God ? I only hope that we should act as decently as the best of our forebears, who, except in the fury of actual combat, did for the most part temper their deeds to use, rather than to destruction. Spencer had no doubt that the needed Reform was impossible without the restoration of Order by the Sword. How sickeningly familiar this sounds but to Spencer it was simple sense and yet his disregard of delegated responsibility can only be understood on grounds of fear. Fear, as the father of cruelty, echoed down our history through the wholesale massacres of Cromwell to the complete conquest of William III. Spencer's most constructive recommendations are embodied in his lively dialogue, dated circa 1596, between

NOT ONLY DID THEY SPEAK A FOOLISH FOREIGN LANGUAGE, BUT THEY WORE WHAT ANY REASONABLE PERSON MUST CONSIDER TO BE ABSURD CLOTHES, AND A PREPOSTEROUS HAIR CUT

Iraeneus, representing Spencer, who is interrogated by
Eudoxus.

Hear Eudoxus :
> "What is this you say of so many that remain English
> of them ?
> Why ? Are not they that were once English, English
> still ? "

Iraeneus :
> " No, for some of them are degenerated and growne almost
> more Irish, yea, and more malitious to the English than the
> Irish themselves."

Eudoxus :
> " What heare I ? and is it possible that an Englishman,
> brought up in such sweet civilitie as England affords, should
> find such a liking in that barbarious rudeness that he should
> forget his own nature and forgoe his own nation ? How may
> this bee ? or what (I pray you) may be the cause thereof ? "

Iraeneus :
> " So much can liberty and ill examples do ! . . . . for
> they are more stubborne and disobedient to the law and gov-
> ernment than the Irish be."

Eudoxus :
> (suitably horrified) " In truth Iraeneus, this is more than
> I ever heard, that any English there should bee worse than
> the Irish ! Lord, how quickly doth that country alter one's
> nature ! . . . . ."

Instead of referring to his thesis, it is likely that the
ex-English living in Ireland might find a more congenial
reflection of the " poets' poet " and his sympathy with the
country in his golden stanzas, born of the blood-drenched
Munster in which he lived so many formative years.*
For lively prose Spencer was surpassed by Edmund
Campion writing some twenty years before him. His
history opens : " What variety of choyce matters the
affaires of this Kingdom doe afford to an historian " —
We are off and the pace keeps up. Finally he pleads
indulgence — " howsoever the privilege of an history
hath tempered mine inke with sweet or soure ingredients."

*To those interested, some of the most typical are in the *Faerie Queene*,
Book VI canto iv, 3.

He was strangely perceptive. " The people are thus inclined : religious, franke, amorous, irefull . . . delighted
with warres . . . they follow the dead corpses to the grave
with howlings and barbarous outcries, they are sharp
witted, capable of any studies where they bend themselves . . . greedy for prayse they be and fearful of dis-
pleasure." Would any Irishman to-day scorn this as
ungenerous ? Like Spencer, Campion deplores the
tendency of the English " to wax Irish " but he reveals
his own national confidence when he blandly states after
noting some of their faults, " It may appear how much
Ireland is beholding to God for suffering them to be
conquered, whereby many of these enormities were cured
and more might be would themselves be plyable." —
Plyable !

After he had finished his History, Campion went to
Douai, became a Roman Catholic and a professed Jesuit.
He needed neither the persuasions of his many friends nor
the frightful arguments of three ordeals by torture. He
was hanged at Tyburn in 1581.

The convictions of this band of men is humbling to read
of. In their policy of order by the sword they really did
stress Order and Civilitie ! Yet no minority, however
superior it may believe itself to be, can ultimately control
a majority. It was the forcing of the establishment of a
minority rule, which persisted for 400 years after them,
that constituted the Elizabethan fallacy in Ireland and
by which their descendants are still circumscribed to-day.

The force of their personality survives them and one
may follow their influence in the figures of the great
opposition of Grattan, who was supported by another
Lawrance Parsons of direct Elizabethan line.

Chapter II

LAWRENCE PARSONS, R.A.

It was perfectly appropriate to its time that the writer of Irish pre-first-War memories should have been born in London and have had as her father a Captain in the Royal Artillery. Ireland was at that time completely under Crown Rule and Anglo-Irishmen were proportionately far more heavily represented in the Army and Navy than were their English counterparts. The reason was largely financial since it was cheaper to live in the services if you enjoyed serving overseas. Anglo-Irish country gentlemen had neither coal, railways, nor industrial sites to exploit and their rentals had begun their catastrophic fall. There were a few Castle appointments and they sometimes took in each other's washing by becoming land agents — targets at times for their employers' dissatisfied tenants — but, if they were to keep up even the smallest place for three generations, the only possible hope was to marry money. Looking around it is pleasant and impressive to record how many nice suitable Englishwomen appeared and happily filled the bill. These unions were invariably cocooned in Settlements — astonishingly so to their English co-signatories. Entails sprouted complicated jointures which distorted much of the nuptial blessing and mortgages became the sole resource of the baffled owner. No wonder that young men craved to get away from it all to a job that offered the chance of meeting girls, of sport, and an open air life to which they had been reared. My father had no place to maintain or mortgage to combat and so little private means that he even had to borrow the cost of his " Jacket " to join the Royal Horse Artillery. Only son and fourth child of an unpractical scholar who read Horace as a recreation, he had been brought up at a small place near Birr, close friends of his four cousins who were the sons of the Castle. These contemporaries remained lifelong friends. I was married from the house of one of them and was goddaughter of another. Being well off themselves, they had been concerned as to how Lawrence would surmount his financial shortcomings and subsequently derived keen personal pleasure when he prospered in his profession and kept up the family name. They were all four to become men of ability. Lawrence, the eldest, was a noted astronomer and F.R.S. and Charles, the youngest, was famed for his invention of the steam turbine. All helped their father, Lord Rosse, to construct what was for many years the biggest telescope in the world. They and the estate staff formed the 6ft. reflector with local labour. My father always regretted that instead of joining the cousins in the work he was more attracted by building and sailing boats and in training other small boys to become soldiers.

As a boy he was a competent classical scholar and rendered his Latin with a local Irish pronunciation that would now be much admired, but which, when he arrived at an English public school, was considered unintelligible and placed him at the bottom of his class. Fortunately the Head Master paid the class a surprise visit and after a few questions my father, like the little boy in the fairy story, found himself at the top. His mathematics were as poor as his other subjects were strong, but he always felt it was a triumph that he succeeded in passing out of the " Shop " (Woolwich) without scoring a single mark in that vital subject. Moreover his aggregate was high enough to give him the choice of " Sappers ". Preferring

to be an Artillery man his selection left the Engineer
vacancy for Lord Kitchener below him. No young man
could have started his career in happier vein. All his
life he had a genius for popularity and was immediately
the " fashion " and known as " Beau P.". Riding a penny
farthing bicycle or drinking beer in a long measure " by
the yard ", he looked as carefree as he felt. The Army
had not been ever thus for the impecunious, but Cardwell
and others had recently brought in their reforms. I have
a letter written to Lawrence by his father as he obtained
his commission, circa 1869, in which he writes " how much
easier all this is going to be for you."

RIDING A PENNY FARTHING BICYCLE, HE LOOKED AS CAREFREE AS
HE FELT.

Army reforms had not only been deep, they were wide
and, curiously enough, no place was more drastically
affected than Ireland. When, after the Crimean War,

the army cadre in England was reformulated, instead of barracks being placed strategically alongside important towns, they were removed from industrial centres. Large resident camps were formed near which areas of cheap waste land were available.

After the Boer War I stayed in a charming old house in Hampshire previously belonging to an old Colonel. His son told me that after the Mutiny his father, disgruntled, resigned his commission and bought this nice little place, where he boasted he need never see a soldier again. The address was the Manor House, Aldershot.

Ireland, where rough land was cheaper still, was ideal for these new concentrations, notably at the Curragh. County Cork became the next centre, with Kilworth nearby for manoeuvres. Soon we were in proportion to our numbers much more heavily garrisoned than England. Before the Crimea only light forces were stationed in small barracks or redoubts. Troops then did not form part of the Irish social system.

The new barracks which now shot up followed a familiar plan and comfortable little towns like Fermoy, Athlone and Clonmel benefited by the trade and social life which followed the drum. The barracks were all in the form of quadrangles, topped with a neat clock tower as sole architectural focus. Surrounding hard, weedless squares, they were walled in and approached through important granite-framed gates. An isolated Guard Room kept watch. Behind the main buildings of the self-contained unit were the married quarters, school, gymnasium and Church. Let no one think these alien forces were unpopular, despite outside political rumblings. The districts chosen prospered through the trade and social life which blossomed in the area. House property boomed, farmers found handy markets for forage and root crops.

The troops got on, as Englishmen always have got on with residents of all classes. Local Militia battalions, training with regular units, were well filled. The fashion spread by which practically every country gentleman of any standing acquired military rank. Talk of Prussia !

By the time the forces were well settled throughout Ireland, the close association of the officer class with the civilians of like minds created and encouraged a Loyalist standpoint which no other influence could have created. The women were quite as much impressed as their men, perhaps even more so. Compare their lot with that of rectors' daughters in rural England, or even in larger country towns. The manpower on tap for dances, theatricals, picnics, tennis was ample and obliging. The better-to-do Roman Catholic families were not slow in responding to the magnet. It was only a convinced anti-Britisher who could hold off his daughters from associating with these fascinating creatures, so kind and well turned out, and so ready to enjoy themselves. And the bands and the marquees ! The British officer class ranged from the smartest and most expensive units of the Army to the less endowed " departments ". There was always a cross section of civilians waiting for a military one which was anxious to respond. Many marriages followed and this confusing connection survives in numerous classes in Ireland to-day.

The surplus Irish doctors eagerly accepted the opportunities offered by joining the R.A.M.C. and their work for that service has bridged religion and politics as few other factors can have done.

My father did not serve in Ireland for several years after he joined the Army. As a subaltern at Weedon he had as fellow officer that tragic figure, the Prince Imperial. It used to astonish his English friends that this eccentric

young man, although now in the British army, should
remain "so French". He was extremely slight and as
active as a monkey. After a Guest Night he would go
to his bedroom and get into bed between the sheets, spurs
and all and make the others sit on him. He would then
wriggle out between bed and wall and reappear from
under the bed. He was obsessed and excited with the
desire to see active service and got himself sent to South
Africa. In Zululand he was put in sole charge of a
brother officer but he managed to elude him and rushed
off on his own, to be trapped in an ambush and pierced
by a dozen assegais. The sensitive army honour of those
days abhorred a man who had failed in his trust and yet
lived himself. Recalling the poor Prince's agility and
determination, one feels sympathy with the unlucky officer
who failed to keep him in view, but so general and strongly
was this "heroic" viewpoint held that the unfortunate
man had to leave the Army. The last Napoleon now lies
in that strangely lighted mausoleum at Farnborough,
surrounded by English soldiers in camps around.

Lawrence's next Station, India, was strictly in line with
the usual course of military life. I do not think it is
dogmatic to say that the army Indian complex coloured
much of the attitude which ex-soldiers brought home to
Ireland when eventually they retired to settle down. I
know how deeply this early experience influenced my
father, more so than did his spell out there later as a
General. When he went as a young man to Lucknow
the Mutiny was hot in mind and the site alive with tragic
memories, blunders, friendships and betrayals. The
thought of English soldiers and — worse in the heroic
mood of those days — women and children subjected to
an appalling ordeal cut into his soul. Never again must
such things be ! Because he was essentially humane he

had no thought of oppression but he pledged himself to the ideal of strength " for India's sake as much as for Britain's ". John Nicholson became his hero ; he used to describe to me how Nicholson fired a shot through the tent where he lay wounded to show that he was still alive ; and would tell of the shrine where he was worshipped by the Frontiersmen who served under him. Soldiers in India must be fair, humane and respected, but to keep the peace they must be on top. It was not the English civilians who kept India. They only administered it. Without the Army there could not be strength — and the Indians, like the Irish, understood and admired strength.

And so when the old soldiers came home and sat together in the Kildare Street Club it was impossible for them not to compare the Irish with the Indian situation. The Irish too should be treated kindly, fairly, led, not bullied. Agitators were the curse of both countries. Home Rule was the invention of disloyal fanatics or of paid agitators who only wanted to pull the Empire down.

It was all quite simple.

By the early eighties, after several years of pleasant inexpensive sport, my father had saved enough from the Indian Government, then responsible for paying the British army in India, to take an exchange home and be married.

CHAPTER III

FLORENCE GRAVES.

My mother, Florence, youngest child of Dr. Robert Graves, F.R.S., was a born radical. How it came about I do not know. Her most conventional and decorous mother, Anna (*née* Grogan of Slaney Park, Baltinglass), certainly never alluded to the family rebel, Cornelius, of Johnstown Castle, Co. Wexford, whose end was tactfully passed over in Burke as " died in 1798," while his respectable ensign brother is recorded as " fell " in the same year at the battle of Arklow. Coming from a country family, it was a constant irritant to my grandmother that her husband was a doctor. She worked the eminence to which he rose so adroitly that the Lord Lieutenant and his lady actually dined with them in Merrion Square. Still, she could not feel that this *imprimatur* was as enduring as founding a country seat and, before his death, she persuaded him to buy Cloghan Castle, a distinctive Norman keep by the Shannon, near Banagher. I am very glad she did as its proximity to Birr led later to my parents meeting.

The first of my mother's forebears to come to Ireland had been Colonel William Graves in 1650. His son, James, founded the family, afterwards distinguished for no less than seven admirals including Nelson's Thomas Graves and Lord Graves of the Chesapeake. Henry, the other son, had won the nick-name of Harry of the Long Sword. It is said that even when going to Church he never left behind his formidable blade " for fear of the hostility of the Irish Papists ". His great grandson was the respectable Henry Graves, the antiquary.

27

So far from continuing the tradition of the Long Sword, Henry's descendants must number more scholars and divines than any other family I have heard of. Not only did generations of them sweep Trinity College of gold medals but they married the daughters of other gold medallists and, being extremely prolific, have filled columns of the *Dictionary of National Biography* with the names of LL.D.s and Fellows. I once asked a cousin how it was that the Graves appeared to keep their chins up so unerringly and she replied " they always marry people a bit cleverer than themselves ". Included in their matrimonial bag was Von Ranke, the historian.

Bishop Charles Graves, Fellow of Trinity College, Dublin, son of Thomas, F.T.C.D., Dean of Ardfert, 1802, numbered among his sons Alfred, D.Litt., author of " Father O'Flynn ", and his two daughters married Knightly Admirals of the Fleet, keeping up the average of distinction in careers and in marriage.

My grandfather Robert Graves was born in 1796, before the Battle of the Nile and the Irish Rebellion. Between us we span an alarming stretch of history because my mother was born only shortly before his death in 1853 and I appeared latish in her marriage. Robert who was a Fellow of the Royal Society was the Doctor who gave his name to the disease. His statue is in the Hall of the College of Physicians, facing his great contemporary, Sir William Stokes, P.R.C.P.

The Anglo-Irish are so much associated with landlordism, great and small, that a chronicle of their more social and cultural activities provides a humane alternative field. The Cromwellian settlement introduced many families who later obtained real eminence drawn from a different social order from that of most of those of Elizabethan and Stuart origins.

Robert Graves did not long survive as a semi-country gentleman and after his death, in 1853, my grandmother left Dublin and moved down to Cloghan Castle with " little Flo ", ten years younger than any of her other children.

My mother's account of those days included : reading the classics in the worst of light concealed under heavy furniture ; of the sound of the maid's vanishing footsteps down the stone spiral steps from the attic bedroom where she was crying herself to sleep from fright ; of the happy Sunday breakfasts when, instead of plain " stir-about," she was allowed the treat of the top of her mother's boiled egg.   The rest was policemen.   Kind R.I.C. constables

SUNDAY BREAKFASTS WHEN, INSTEAD OF PLAIN " STIR-ABOUT," SHE WAS ALLOWED THE TREAT OF THE TOP OF HER MOTHER'S BOILED EGG.

were her playmates at bird's-nesting and helping her to ride.   Her mother was a harsh landlord and, therefore, under constant " protection ".   My mother, no doubt mindful of the egg top, was fond of the hard, beautiful little woman and hoped that she would not be shot ; but even then felt that, if she were, she richly deserved it.

Her recollection of the poverty in those post-famine years was distressing, but she formed an affection for the people which never left her, though subsequently it was overlaid by social life in Dublin, and after that as a gunner's pretty wife in garrison towns. Her favourite relatives were the Graves cousins and, I think, of these Robert, the friend and biographer of Rowan Hamilton, influenced her taste in literature.

Her mother had no intellectual interests, but a nice taste in *objets d'art,* which she collected with skill. She was disparaged as a worldly ignoramus by the learned Graves family, whose marriages were still enlarging their cultural scope.

The recollection which formed the deepest aversion in my mother's young mind was the intensive evangelical and anti-Roman atmosphere of that day. It had degenerated from its early fire to smouldering embers of intolerance. Well-to-do old ladies collected together, abusing their neighbours and puffing up their own worth as " happy, saved Christians, dear ". Naturally many evangelicals led saintly lives, including my mother's elder brother, Richard, who was in Orders in England.

Among the professed evangelicals was my mother's great Aunt Arabella, sister of my great grandfather " Pentateuch " Graves, a dreadful old tatar, who used to force the small child to " repeat her hymn ", under penalty of Hell for failure. Once the child's brother, William, a fast young man, taught her a new verse, gave her a shilling, and told her to " repeat this hymn to Aunt Bella ". He waited at the keyhole. Poor little Flo did her bit :

" Damn your eyes, if ever you tries
   To rob a poor man of his beer."
Great Aunt Bella could not trust Hell to deal with such
enormity. Little Flo got a severe whacking on earth.
William, a thoroughly nasty piece of work, just ran off
and left her !

Shortly after she grew up, her mother died and
Cloghan Castle passed to William, who had two sons.
The elder and godly Richard had died leaving an only
daughter, but to my grandmother's ambition the male
line mattered most and Richard's daughter was passed
over. She married into the family of J. M. Synge.

Beyond being an army racquets champion, William
has left nothing for his family to remember ; his two
very nice sons died without heirs and eventually Cloghan
Castle was sold by William's widow. At the auction my
mother bought a huge *famille verte* bowl, looted from the
Imperial Palace at Pekin, which a grateful patient had
given to Robert Graves. It is the only souvenir I have
of my grandfather and it now roosts where I write.

My mother then lived with her eldest sister, Georgina,
twenty years her senior, and wife of Edward Blackburne,
Q.C., of Rathfarnham Castle, Co. Dublin. Uncle Edward
was a dear old man, who liked being left alone playing
the organ in the huge draughty ballroom. One evening
he was interrupted by the arrival of a friend who explained that he was interested in a device for pushing air
into rubber, so useful for bicycle wheels. He had come
to ask the old gentleman to help to finance him. Uncle
Edward, who was slow and cautious, was horrified and
begged his friend to drop hair-brained schemes and stick
to his own work. Fortunately Harvey Ducros and the
northern inventor, Mr. Dunlop, had better luck elsewhere,
but how many people realise Dublin's share in this

wheeled revolution ?   Still I am sorry for my cousins who
succeeded Uncle Edward.

Rathfarnham was a majestic, grim pre-Georgian house,
once owned by the Elys, Loftus family.   Its ceilings were
painted by Angelica Kaufmann ; its furniture was period
French ; its dinner service was silver.   Moreover there
was an unnerving ghost, who clanked around with his
sword, seeking for his ladylove whose bones had been
found and removed from the thick walls.   Several of my
cousins saw him.

My aunt, Georgina, inherited her mother's hard core
and very sound intelligence.   When young she entertained in the grand manner and when widowed ran
the estate admirably and profitably, but she was a miser
on the same scale, monumental rather than just stingy.
If she is remembered without affection, at least she retains
the respect which all outstanding personalities command.

Her grandson sold the property in lots before the first
war and Jesuits now occupy the Castle, whilst suburban
golfers negotiate the bunkers alongside the Dodder river
where I used to watch my cousin fish.   Villas now vie
with each other in amenities as they fringe the boundary
between the two sets of pompous gateways.

I cannot think which of the purchasers — villas or
Castle — my Aunt Georgina would have disliked the
more.   But the price was good.

I never slept at the Castle.   I think my mother was
suspicious that I might hear something frightening from
" the maids ".   She herself was not psychic but later she
told me of times when her little dog cringed in corners
with its hair standing on end.   When Aunt Georgina's
daughter was married and the family centred there for
the festivities, my cousin Hubert described to me the
night before, when his bedroom door opened and the un-

happy soldier, in full 18th Century uniform, marched down the steps, crossed the room and left by the opposite door. Hubert had subsequently not spent a sleepful night and at dawn he had drifted to the window and beheld — hareing down the avenue — the hired man from Hills' Restaurant making a terrified exit. He had taken nothing of the Castle's contents, or his wedding party pay. He had just seen too much !

During my mother's Rathfarnham visits I used to stay in Dublin with my aunts, Father's kind, fat, unintellectual sisters, who chiefly existed to overfeed us on a diet my mother deplored as being " too rich for either of you ". He and I used to sit back to back on the top of the horse bus from Terenure to Rathfarnham, counting the White Horses still displayed in the fanlights over the front doors. These, I am sure, had a genteel rather more than a political significance and I wish I could still spot a few from the new Juggernaut buses as they sway past.

Chapter IV

NORA PARSONS.

Slightly buttressed by economies made in India, my father was now able to marry but a further economical spell was started with a Volunteer command. After six years, my arrival threatened further complications and he applied for his majority to be in Garrison Artillery, being cheaper. He was duly gazetted to Jamaica.

En route for this trans-Atlantic trip, I was brought for my first visit to Ireland to be inspected by various relations. I understand that my cries at my grandmother's old home in Co. Wicklow were loud enough to be heard in Co. Carlow, where I now write.

It is impossible to know when one actually begins to remember and we returned to England from Jamaica when I was four, but I retain a few vivid impressions of Newcastle in the Blue Mountains and one of Kingston, the Port. I remember our hut at Newcastle and the row of kindly negro servants. This hut was ideally convenient for Globe Trotters, as they used to be called, and my parents were expected to entertain these well-to-do strangers who regarded accepting the hospitality as conferring a privilege on the hosts. Froude, the historian, wrote in his " Impressions " that they lunched with an intelligent Artillery officer and his smiling Irish wife. My mother was indignant at the limitation of the compliment !

My parents loved Jamaica and the easy life — they rode everywhere, wearing pyjamas that concealed and protected evening dress.

Another Irishman, Sir Henry Blake, was then Governor of the Island. His wife was the daughter of a well-known society wit, the affluent Mr. Bernal Osborne, whose elder daughter had married the Duke of St. Albans.

On our way home we stayed with them at King's House, before I was four years old. Sir Henry, like so many Irishmen, rose to the top of the Colonial Service. When he retired they bought Myrtle Grove at Youghal, once residence of Raleigh and Lawrence Parsons. At the time when my father was in command in Cork we used to visit them there, admire the Chinese curios and look at Lady Blake's skilful botanical paintings.

From Jamaica we spent a year at Woolwich, where one day an old lady in a carriage was pointed out to me and I was told to remember that I had seen Queen Victoria. I do remember quite well ; she passed me from right to left.

I WAS TOLD TO REMEMBER THAT I HAD SEEN QUEEN VICTORIA.

At Woolwich there was an absurd late echo from Jamaica. My parents had promised Lady Blake that they would visit her sister in London. Duly the ducal invitation to lunch arrived, my parents smartened themselves up and left me in charge of my dashing cousin Hubert, he who was to see the Rathfarnham ghost. History repeated itself in the form of a white rabbit, present from the little boy next door. It took as vicious a tit-bit from my finger as once a monkey had done. Of course, cousin Hubert's new ulster bore the brunt of the flow as I clung to his shoulder. He tried to drown my yells by shouting his views of parents who lunched with duchesses. The little boy from next door had an eccentric taste for dolls and gave me a pair of drawers from one he considered overdressed. He became Sir Dudley North, Admiral of the Home Fleet.

The end house of the small group of three was occupied by another man who rose to distinction, Sir Harry Sclater, Q.M.G. in War I. Lady Sclater had been a Bartelot from Sussex and her brother was then serving on the staff of Stanley's African Expedition. Harry Sclater told my father he had carefully noted down the vivid telepathic vision his wife had experienced early one morning when she distinctly saw her brother murdered from a shot by a half-caste, as he stood outside a native kraal. Three months later Stanley's despatch admitted the death.

My father was appointed to command the 67th Battery R.F.A. at Fermoy, so from Woolwich we moved to Southern Ireland which I did not leave for nine years. Those of my upbringing who spent their youth in Victoria's reign remember a social Ireland which the two past generations would barely recognize. Distances and slower transport made what appeared static even more so. We formed part of the centre of that circle on which the sun never set. To us, loyalty combined King, Country, religion, one's personal safety, one's family's property and, above all, one's class. Upon class depended status and any fun that was going. The sense of loyal superiority was recognized and cherished down to the Protestant charwoman, copying her betters, whose scorn of her R.C. opposite would be uninhibited. To have questioned, let alone defied, this acceptance of loyalty would have meant social extinction, but nobody did except once, when the most beautiful woman of them all, Maude Gonne, daughter of a Cavalry Colonel, " lost her head " before the Boer War.

From the early nineties my father was stationed consecutively in Fermoy, Limerick, Athlone and Cahir and those barrack squares were the context of my childhood. At Fermoy, where we occupied the top of the house, I used to lie on my regimental iron bed in the early summer mornings where, by a visual freak, I could see the red coats of the infantry drilling below on the white limestone gravel. Red shapes were thrown up as blurry shadows on the ceiling. They swayed uncertainly over my head ; bugles blew below and I was quite sure that the French, always the French, were invading us. It is strange how well one remembers anything frightening. My other fear was passing the regimental stag of the Seaforth Highlanders, which was kept in the guard-room by the entrance gate. It was a depressed cynical beast, lonesome for the distant glens and it leered at me with a hostile eye.

No other Major before my father had dreamt of occupying the married quarters to which he was entitled. The separate C.O.'s house was the perquisite of the Colonel commanding the infantry battalion which shared the barracks with the 67th Battery. However, as my mother had determined that my father was going to hunt,

adequate economy had to be made. The house was one
in the middle of the Square and the Major's rooms
occupied the three floors above those where the Battery
wheeler plied his craft. One climbed a flight of
stairs, covered with the bristliest coconut matting,
leading to the hall-door and sitting-rooms. Above that
were the bedrooms, but the *chef d'oeuvre* was the top floor
with kitchen, my room and an E.C. It was all most
handy. The soldier servant used to put apple fritters
under my pillow on his way down to the dining-room and
as for the E.C., what child of really sensitive feeling
would not have preferred a troop of moustached soldiers
to " do what was necessary " rather than a noisy creaking
" Niagara ". We loved Fermoy but to suggest that it
introduced me to anything Irish but the scenery is absurd.
The barracks dominated my outlook except for the visits
I paid with my mother to large and bitterly cold country
houses. Even there a British military milieu was only
exchanged for a rigidly Anglo-Irish country atmosphere.
" The child " was anxiously watched in case she were
already acquiring a brogue ; alarmingly, she was found
to be adept at placing bets on the 3.30, primed by the
soldier servant. However, my father was finding the role
of being bookie so expensive that he called it off and the
art I had acquired withered away.

   With so many relatives my holidays were spent in
different country houses, identified by the fruits in season.
Looking back they did not seem whimsically Irish, but
beautifully ordered by English and Scottish upper
servants, who were driven to the C. of I. in wagonettes
on Sunday. I thank my parents for their mercy in sparing
" the child " those long ante-Communion, plus Litany,
with Sermon, Services. I was used to a brisk three
quarters of an hour Garrison Service, with father timing

the sermon as an Officer should. Bass voices lustily rendered the hymns.

It was surely one of the least pleasant aspects of those days that any child of my world must have regarded religion as the most obvious class distinction. The R.C. underservants did not even have the wagonette. They balanced, if they drove at all, on the second best Irish car.

This device of using religion as a social lever is so little known in England that it is hard to realise. There, some of the most distinguished of her aristocratic families have retained the old Faith. It would have astonished the generation of my childhood to be told that in France the aristocrats regarded the remaining Huguenots as hopelessly bourgeois. The particular factor here was, of course, political and has now disappeared. Religious differences remain a constant but not as much a snob factor.

Before the War the wife of a distinguished bishop, after a visit to the North, complained to me how narrowminded they were there. She further said that a Northern bishop's wife had asked her : " Of course all your servants are Protestant ? ". I said, " Oh no ! only the uppers." Such an assertion would be comic to-day.

Hardly any memory of those distant days is concerned with Ireland or the Irish ; of course, our soldier servant was English and so was my nurse-cum-housemaid, who married him. Garrison life enveloped us completely. I remember no truly Irish impact unless one mentions the nice daily governess (she had only the lightest Cork lilt). It was through her, Miss Clancy, who dutifully taught me " Little Arthur's History of England ", that I first sensed a small difference. By mistake a ham sandwich was given to her one Friday and *she spat it out* ! I was overcome by this wonderful tribute to Faith.

Naturally all military events thrilled me. I collected regimental badges and buttons and knew everything about the 67th Battery. It had been top of the annual practice and so the men wore an embroidered laurel badge on their collars. My father's four sergeants, whom he encouraged to hunt on government chargers, beat the Xth Hussars at the Curragh Gymkhana and who could forget the V.C. races at the Garrison Sports ? What more had life got ? When the Battery was moved to Limerick, by my eighth birthday, the change only seemed to present a new venue for further glorious events.

I was now old enough to make my own friends instead of meekly accepting the children of my parents' friends and can remember fascinating Christmases inspired by hostesses who had learnt the exciting technique in Germany and where Christmas Eve was almost as good as the real thing. One friend was Noel Furlong, who in the course of time owned and trained Reynoldstown which, ridden by Noel's son, Frank, twice won the Grand National under his colours.

At Limerick the barracks were smaller and more friendly, moreover we had a detached house, but before we moved in my mother and I were invited to stay at the Palace with the Bishop, then Charles Graves, Gold Medallist and first cousin of my grandfather. It was a surprise to my father to find that this old Dresden china piece knew more about modern gunnery than he did. Graves was an outsize mathematician and left his impact, not only on his generation, but on his family after him. His ten children nearly all won fame themselves or through their children. I do not know whether Robert, poet and novelist, feels more indebted to his grandfather, the old Bishop, or to his most charming mother, daughter of Von Ranke the historian. Anyhow this clutch of

divines and blossoms of literature were unexpected consequences of their Cromwellian forebear, the Colonel of
the Long Sword. I am sure that the first, or nearly the
first, Director of the B.B.C., Cecil Graves, was equally
beholden to the Bishop as he was to his maternal uncle,
Sir Edward Grey, whom he succeeded at Falloden.

The barracks were, as I described, tucked away and
only reached through a slum. At night came the pigs,
processions of them, squealing, poor creatures, on their
last patrol to Shaw's Bacon Factory. What makes more
row than one pig under a gate ? . . . . Of the hideous
poverty and degradation of the slums between the railway
station and the barracks at Limerick my father had much
to say. The battery route marches, the date was well on
in the 90s, had to be diverted from that road as naked
women fought in the streets and faction fights drew blood.
Such dreadful people indeed !

In 1937 when my husband was Adviser to the Limerick
City Manager on their new Town Plan, I told the latter
of these recollections and he drove me round to see the
tidy bourgeous community that now occupies the area.
It is sympathetic for intellectuals to make merry over the
ninety and nine just persons who people the suburbs ;
one forgets that the unconventional can become equally
smug.

Although my father had always professed not to have
wanted a son, he brought up his only child as half an able
bodied seaman and half an early pioneer. We tied reef
knots, spliced ropes and made fires and wigwams, de-
spising the incompetent. I don't know how I ever got
over it. Perhaps I didn't. With the vast Shannon beside
us, the soldier groom took me fishing when my father
couldn't come and I can still see a flat fish looking like
a soup plate dangling from my rod. On Sundays he and

I lived on the Quays gazing at sailing ships and memorising their rigs. There were numbers of them then in Limerick. When it was raining I sat on my father's knee and he read round the pictures in Dickens and sometimes, as a great treat, Mayne Reid and " Masterman Ready " at which father always cried. They were not cynics then and genuine tears were on ready tap. I was deeply attached to my mother but she wasn't " one of Us ". She was a bit of a butterfingers. She just couldn't tie a reef knot, she was prone to sprain her ankle and I did not then fully appreciate her genius when she fell, as she frequently did, of rolling over like a hedgehog instead of trying to save herself. In later years I have longed to acquire this art. Her one athletic talent was riding and I disliked horses. It was not until she was a much older woman that I fully perceived all we owed her, though my father had the good sense to realise it before.

A SHAKY IRISH JAUNTING CAR, BEARING ON ONE SEAT A SMALL BRIGHT YELLOW COFFIN AND ON THE OTHER A SHAWLED WOMAN.

A final memory, only a flash, outside Limerick. I was up on the high foot-path and there passed by me a shaky Irish jaunting car, bearing on one seat a small bright yellow coffin and on the other a shawled woman. The driver sat in front, hunched and indifferent with baggy reins. Continuously the single mourner " keened ", a banshee wail of woe. I wish Jack Yeats had seen it and also had seen the fat prosperous little girl, standing moon-faced looking on.

Chapter V

CROWN RAMPANT.

I spent my tenth birthday at Athlone where my father, now Lieutenant-Colonel, had been posted. This was the first real improvement in our fortunes. Apart from the better pay there had been a blessed legacy, an entirely unexpected one, from an elderly and not very close cousin, just because " she had always liked Lawrence ", as so many people did. Only those who have known stringent economies for years can realise the release from anxiety that this windfall made for my parents. Old pre-war days are often cited as the golden era for a " certain class ". For some of them, yes, but I doubt if at any period of English social life there were more difficult contrasts and adjustments ; so many people were not in-dependent, and keeping up with the Cholmondeleys was much more exhausting even than panting after the Jones — schools, clubs, regiments, all had to be buttressed by dividends or allowances — there were few incomes at hand to be earned. Unfair differences in the same family were often flagrant.

Even clothes cost more before obliging " pegs " appeared to provide good cuts and materials. It is not surprising that in those days Ireland should have attracted a considerable inflow of English retired Service people on small pensions. These new-comers reinforced the local Anglo-Irish gentry of much the same circumstances in intense Crown Loyalty. It was not a circle in which intellectual ferment worked its disturbing influence and in return for blessings received, its members gave un-stinted service in two Wars and unbroken, if often tactless,

44

resistance to nationalist upheavals during the Troubles. Founded when garrison town life made a Mrs. Bennett paradise for its daughters, an element of this settlement still survives. Paradoxically it is personally popular in the new Eire and often inhabits the same " nice little places " it had acquired early in the century. The appeal of this settlement was strongest in the smaller towns. Limerick then had its larger social hinterland and only " called " on those it knew. Like Fermoy, social Athlone became an extension of garrison life.

In Athlone the Colonel's house was detached with a good garden and it seemed to me to possess every amenity that Earth, or Heaven for that matter, could provide. These included an iron pipe forming a chimney to an out-building. My father had obligingly made me a sling and for hours I practised aiming stones until one day I really did hit the chimney. I can remember nothing else in life that gave me a purer sense of achievement. The blissful freedom was interrupted when a nice young English resident governess was engaged. Later she told us that the first look at the child standing defiant, sling in hand, tempted an immediate retreat. Actually she remained a devoted friend until I was sent to Heathfield and she became engaged to be married. Considering how greatly " Willie " was beloved by my parents it amazes me, looking back, to think what a poor social time she was given. No share indeed of Mrs. Bennett's paradise. My mother invited her to every engagement at which it was then possible to have your governess but these were limited. An unwritten invisible bar absolutely defined the status. If the girl were older things were easier as she could take a natural share in the elders' interests. But " Willie " was only twenty-four and I can still see her looking out of the schoolroom window at the glass roofed gymnasium where the light shone and the band could be heard playing the latest. " I can't bear it," my mother would say as she pulled on her long white gloves. Had she flouted prejudice she could not have been sure that Willie would have secured partners — she was neither strikingly pretty nor quite smart enough — and matters might have been worse. Moreover the Blue Buffs — or whatever the host regiment was — had, naturally, not included her in the invitation. Her outings were restricted to those house-holds with children of my age. Near starvation was the only motive that could induce any girl of spirit to become a governess, and school teacher seemed only one degree better.

Pre-Boer War girls frequently enjoyed the exciting stimulus of becoming " High Church ". Willie, of course, was very High, and the C. of I. was a continual affront to her. I remember her amazement when my father, after hearing her description of a Beautiful Service at Brighton when they led in a donkey to head a Palm Sunday procession, suddenly said : "But damn it, my dear, I always thought that Our Lord was such a simple kind of cove ". " Colonel ! " " Well, I'm sorry, my dear - -" " Don't mind him Willie ", from my mother.

Until I was ten years old memories were thin and less vivid but now they fairly crowd into my head and the job is to select a few that may have some bearing on my theme. The garrison world still predominates and the social circle not only surrounds it but is integral to its life. Only the particular environment of scenery isolates itself and creates a context that is essentially its own. The Roscommon bogs with their distant sunsets, the whiffs of turf, and the rare but dramatic figures silhouetted against the sky contrast with the snugger Westmeath, east of the Shannon, bordering the edge of Lough Rea. Even the

river had its garrison angle because of the artillery yacht
" The Meercham ", on which we made those wonderful
expeditions among the many islands of Lough Rea.
Probably the impelling fascination of the Irish scenery
has done more than any other influence to bring those
reared here — and who really love it — into its unity. In
all the stations where I was " quartered " as a child I can
remember certain pet spots where I was rooted in wonder
and where, if I pass them to-day, the same overwhelming
visual nostalgia overpowers me. This may not be patriotism but it is something deeper and more possessive.
Coming home from overseas the sight of the Dublin Bay
Coast is gripping and makes the English countryside —
lovely as it is — foreign to us who are claimed by the far
off hills or the stony, furzy fields. Edith Somerville
describes an Irish concert as the map of Ireland set to
music but the usual trite lines one hears there are forgiven
when one recalls the reality behind them. It is tempting to
speculate on how much the open views have affected the
dwellers of the " Celtic fringe " in comparison with the
effect on its snug occupants of the closed warm hearth of
England's " Home, Sweet Home ". Driving through
Athlone a few years ago, I was glad to see that the
Barracks were still there. The Officer in Charge took me
around and I had a real wallow in remembered details.
The pleasant relations between the old British and the
Irish Army is one of those — perhaps unexpected —
things that makes life gracious.

The spacious Drill Field of our days is now a golf
course, indeed even then it was often so used. It was on
May 24th that it blossomed into glory and became the
stage for the Queen's Birthday Full Dress parade. My
father would groan as he fitted on his tight tunic and
drew the belt in. How much I resented his gunner blue

instead of lovely showy infantry scarlet, but his Sabretache of heavy gold lace and the *Ubique* monogram was a consolation. Then the guns saluted and the bands played and the ladies got out of their carriages and dog carts and stood stiffly upright for the Anthem beneath their gay parasols. Of course, one was Loyal ! In the bright midday light the Roscommon Bog on the horizon seemed flat and remote.

On the Great Day of the Diamond Jubilee in '97 I was for some reason left alone. It was piping hot but I staged my private demonstration, dressed in a toy breastplate and helmet, made in Germany. I shoulder-armed my wooden rifle and leading my dog by a red, white and blue riband marched a prescribed three rounds of our large garden. At the end of the second round, I drew up. I was thirsty and scorched by the hot sun. The dog looked at me appealingly but " Britons ", and we were

WE FINISHED THE THIRD ROUND, BOTH TAILS UP.

indeed Britons then, " never, never . . . ." We finished
the third round, both tails up.

The following year, for the first time in my life, I
realised that there was an undercurrent of events. Every
young civilian in the place wore a white china button in
his cap, bearing the ominous legend : " Remember '98."
" What ", I asked, " was '98 ? ". *Little Arthur's History*
had never mentioned it. It was told that it was an awful
Rebellion and that it was a great pity that they were
digging all that up again. There were so many of these
young men and, as they wore the buttons all through the
year, I began to feel a bit scared. But after all one got
used to it and anyway they were only common fellows.
Compare them with the lovely soldiers, the brass bands
and father's Sabretache !

There were fewer large houses with Protestant staffs
near Athlone, but the hospitality to the garrison was as
pressing as ever and the balance of social power was the
same.

A charming old cousin of my mother's lived at Auburn
House, near the Sweet Village of that name. This was
more a square dignified home than a country seat and it
was not difficult to picture Goldsmith when you had read
the " Deserted Village " and walked about the plain
surrounding it.

To my father sport came a long way ahead of games
but it was at Athlone that I first discovered that I had an
" eye ". The place abounded in game fiends, so much so
that my mother, who also had an " eye " but no physique,
found she was always being insulted because she was not
better. The Barracks Gymnasium was filled by local
badminton fans and a small band of experts had no
patience with those who could not hit *hard*. How much
she detested them ! But being, like all children, an un-

sympathetic snob, I was horribly ashamed of her. The
same party excelled at modern croquet, indeed produced
a couple of English champions and I owe it to their
children that I learnt the scope of full sized lawns and
three ball brakes when young. I became only a tolerable
club player at tennis, though a Terror at the Rectory,
but as I had a knack of acquiring good partners I managed
to win more pots throughout my life than my skill merited.
Apart from the fun, a gift for games introduces a player
to a large cross section of people which otherwise would
remain unknown. While the discipline of being able to
win or lose would put a strain on the most ardent advocate
of " IF ", at the best one can but try to appear to be a
good loser. Can one ever really achieve it ? At Athlone
they certainly did not.

I believe now that it was very largely because of the
malaise my mother endured there at badminton and
croquet that she persuaded my father to arrange an exchange between the Commands of Athlone and Cahir in
County Tipperary. To a person attracted by sailing, the
Shannon had obvious advantages ; to one, who preferred
the galloping Tipps, Cahir was a magnet. So to Cahir
we went. Here the locals were mostly hereditary owners
of large houses or had bought them and there were fewer
of the small retired *clientèle* of Athlone. Their sons
joined the richer regiments, they entertained and hunted
in the grand manner and the gunners — there were no
infantry   quartered   there — made   many   profitable
marriages with the neighbours. Altogether the social
atmosphere of a wide neighbourhood was rarer but it
varied not one whit in the perfection of its crowned
loyalty.

There is much more to remember in Cahir and lovely
Tipperary but little that is significant. Lord Roberts,

then C. in C., who had a special appreciation of my father and regretted that he had not had an opportunity of

THE DISCIPLINE OF BEING ABLE TO WIN OR LOSE WOULD PUT A STRAIN ON THE MOST ARDENT ADVOCATE OF "IF."

seeing active service, paid us one of his routine visits. " Now remember ", warned my mother, " he is a very pious and *good* little man. He does not like little girls to be tom-boys or ", after a pained glance, " dirty, so do be ready when you are called for after tea '. I played up so extravagantly well, holding a large copy of *Swiss Family Robinson*, and either casting my glances aloft or drooping them down, that my mother said the effect was nauseating.

A year later Lord Roberts took the opportunity of getting my father appointed to Aldershot where, in the event of war in S. Africa breaking out, he would be among the first to see active service. This was in August '99 and the chance came very soon. Of course, I was excited to see England and I was not fond of the town of Cahir, especially on fair days. Could anything equal the mud and filth of such events, with practically every man drunk at the end ? People, especially educated men and women, may drink more to-day but they do it indoors — or in cars ! To a child the horrors of drunken men lying on the roads cannot be described.

So I was quite glad to go.

Chapter VI

BOER WAR.

We spent only a month in the smart lines of North Camp, Aldershot, where in the C.O.'s Quarters, for the first time, I actually lived in a house with a bathroom. These amenities percolated slowly into Ireland. In Birr Castle they were not installed until well after 1900 ; at my husband's home, though his father reluctantly put in two during the '90s, he refused to use either. No gentleman, he would declare, would wash in a common bath, if he could afford to have his own brought to him.

My father had taken with him as batsmen both my friend of Fermoy and the groom of Limerick. The groom had grown increasingly pompous. " Me and the Colonel " were always cited in that order but in action he proved unexpectedly timorous in keeping appointments. My dear old ally of Fermoy was without shame in letting his tears flow. " I'm shocked at you " said my ex-Nanny, as she clutched young Stanley Clifford ; " Oh ! how will you bear it ", he moaned, " when you read my name on the list of the Slain? " Apparently he went on weeping but, my father said, never scrimped an order either on the way out, when seasick, or under hot fire in Natal. My mother and I lived in that fearsome " Glen Parva " until Ladysmith was relieved by " General Butler, Me, and the Colonel " and the General brought my father home with him to take charge of an artillery practice camp.

During the latter stage of the Ladysmith relief action Butler had promoted him full Colonel commanding all the artillery in his army corps, following the disastrous

53

earlier loss of guns and men when my father's predecessor
had been taken prisoner and Lord Robert's son was killed.
The subsequent strategic use of massed artillery on the
Tugela heights was an innovation and opened the way to
Ladysmith ; this created considerable excitement, and war
correspondents had collected with other interested
observers ; one of the youngest excitedly approached my
father, " Remember, Colonel ", he declared dramatically,
" You are making history ! "   My father had had no
sleep for three nights. He put his eye-glass in his eye and
recognized Winston Churchill. He was beautifully curt :
" Go to Hell ! " I think it was nice of the young man that
when only a few years later he became a Cabinet Minister
and was standing in full regalia at a St. James Levée,
seeing my father, he at once came forward with a friendly
outstretched hand. Father apparently just touched it.
" I don't care for that theatrical type of fellow ", he afterwards explained to me.

I wonder what he would have thought of Press
Conferences !

The Boer War proved, if that were needed, the fighting
fervour of the Irish regiments when they stormed the
Tugela heights.

The half dozen Irish regiments had originally received
their numbers after the disbandments of the Indian cam-
paigns. With their depots in Ireland their recruitment
was excellent only when there was a war on. In peace
time they may have lacked the spit and polish of English
battalions and easily got bored, and therefore drunk.
They were not drawn from the better classes and were a
toughish lot and although popular with the people were
generally, and perhaps naturally, scorned by the Patriot
element. Their officers, though Anglo-Irish, were mostly
Protestant. The Irish achievements in S. Africa caught

the public imagination and led to the old Queen's very courageous decision in 1900 to visit Ireland, after a lapse of a generation of neglect. My mother had always been indignant over her preference for the Highlands. How far the political atmosphere might have been modified by a Royal Residence no one can say. The Patriots believe not at all, but the fact remains that the ordinary people are keenly personal and are enthralled by royal pageantry. They may not recognise the Crown but they will like the wearer. In my lifetime no officials caused as much popular Irish excitement as the Duke of Connaught and his two pretty daughters during his command in Dublin.

The Queen's welcome was not just engineered by Unionists, though admittedly the usual tactless exultation of a few was enough to wreck it. Whatever " patriotic " people may try to make out, all classes (except official politicians) recognised that the old lady wished to express her appreciation of the dead and the courage of the living.

It was a spontaneous and generous act of a very old woman and it was accepted in that spirit by a people quick to recognise what is genuine.

The monumental arch standing in St. Stephen's Green at the Grafton Street end was erected to the memory of those soldiers. Even the bitter taunt " Traitors' Gate " with which it was pilloried did not destroy its significance for the relatives of the many Dublin Fusiliers and other regiments. Their British allegiance was part of the queer mix-up of those days. Those who knew them best realised what good Irishmen they were. Like so many soldiers, they were not enough interested in politics to wish to stay at home. They joined for many and divers reasons, but they were with their pals and when it came to a fight they behaved as gallantly as Irishmen always do.

It would be sad if only an old English Queen were to honour them, and it is equally sad, if inevitable, that their Colours can only rest in the Church of Ireland Cathedrals.

The general and unexpected affection and loyalty of the serving Irish to their Regimental Corps and officers was one of those unexplained contradictions which neither side can fully understand. Naturally it created deep satisfaction to the side that benefited but the lasting bitterness which it provoked among the Nationalist elements is much more difficult to unravel. Amongst the British Indian Regiments there was the same affection and loyalty without the corresponding resentment when the connection ended. Yet admittedly there has been an outstandingly bigger death roll of Irishmen who volunteered for and fell in the Boer and the two World Wars than of the Irish "Martyrs" who died during the Troubles with England. The first lot are not just forgotten by the Nationalists, they are remembered with obloquy. That Irishmen having pledged their word should stick to it is surely a mark of character and honour, and this loyal quality has been the firm foundation on which the new State has been built. It is understandable that serving the enemy against their own side was resented during the Troubles but to keep it up by hating the Dublin Fusiliers who died in the Boer and the First World War seems fantastic. Only the British Legion does them honour on Poppy Day, and how few of the general public in Ireland, even when they would like to, feel it " safe " to wear a poppy !

So the Traitors' Gate remains an English tribute to brave men though, fortunately for its survival after over fifty years, most people have forgotten what it signifies.

But the first World War is more recent and during it

other Irishmen joined the Dublin Fusiliers for what they
believed was Europe's survival. Among those was Tom
Kettle, one of the most brilliant young barristers of his
day, poet, wit and patriot, he stood out among his con-
tempories. His friends honoured him by erecting a bust
in St. Stephen's Green. It was not allowed to stay there
for long. The bust was forcibly removed from the
pedestal bearing his name, which for several years remained an empty and perhaps the more effective witness.
After a while it was hoped that there was a kinder spirit
abroad. The bust was replaced. In 1960, over forty
years after his death, a cold night was chosen and the
very heavy bronze was uplifted once again and the bust
featuring Tom Kettle was dropped into the nearby lake.

Perhaps these so-called Patriots might learn a practical
lesson from their neighbours the ardent Scots. All Scotsmen stick up for gallant Scotsmen rather than for
Nationalist ideals and that is what surely holds them
together in unbroken brotherhood.

After his return from South Africa my father was
appointed Artillery Commandant at Salisbury Plain, and
we went to live in a graceful Queen Anne house by the
Avon. It had belonged to the Poore family and the then
baronet and admiral had married a daughter of Bishop
Graves of Limerick. Throughout my life nothing has
stood out more than the persistent stream of prosperous
Anglo-Irish, breaking through everywhere. Ida Poore
had a neat wit and her sayings used to be quoted by
Queen Victoria when Sir Roger was in command of the
Royal Yacht. " Ma'am, it was a complexion like a new
laid egg ", especially pleased her.

Even the C. in C. at Salisbury, Sir Evelyn Wood, was
connected with home. His family was partly Irish and
his sister was Kitty O'Shea, the Love that wrecked

Parnell's career. He was a lively old man and his daughter, Tory, had the family attraction. On one occasion she helped us to galvanise a dreadfully dull garden party, from which all the military had been deflected by unexpected manoeuvres. After her guests had departed my mother looked in the mirror and settled her hat. She then turned to Tory : " Thank you. You have converted a Saxon funeral into an Irish wake ".

During these years I was at school at Heathfield, Ascot ; it had a snob reputation but my time there was wholly congenial, as my intimates were, of course, Anglo-Irish, a Chenevix-Trench and a daughter of another soldier, Sir George White, whose son, Jack, was an impulsive idealist and left many bright green (and red) friends in Dublin. I owe to Heathfield any taste for culture I ever had. Miss Wyatt, its founder, was a strange uncertain genius, lacking all diplomas, but who opened many windows in young minds.

It sounds too repelling to admit that I played in all the teams and won a strange little prize — for Health.

In 1903 my parents went to India where my father had been appointed to Lord Kitchener's Staff as Inspector General of Artillery. I remained at Heathfield until sent to France to be " finished '. In Paris I watched a hostile crowd melt under the genial smiles of Edward VII and, when I stayed at Dunkirk, was permitted by the conductor to drive an electric tram. During this achievement my unnerved holiday governess tried her best to protest, but even my French was more telling than hers — especially when rendered in a bogus Irish brogue.

A brother-in-law of Miss Wyatt, who was in the French navy, took me over a small French destroyer. The unsuspecting commander kindly showed me their new guns, which were fitted with a special glycerine recoil. After my time at Salisbury Plain I had learnt what to ask for and when my father passed on the information to the Master General of Ordnance in India, he wrote a long list of information for " that intelligent fellow " to find out. Fortunately we had left Dunkirk, or I might have ended in some Bastille.

DURING THIS ACHIEVEMENT MY UNNERVED HOLIDAY GOVERNESS TRIED HER BEST TO PROTEST, BUT EVEN MY FRENCH WAS MORE TELLING THAN HERS

CHAPTER VII

INDIA.

My parents were well settled in by the time I joined them. I went out by sea, and so started my claim to have been sick in every ocean. Their first dinner party before I arrived in Simla, had had its complication. While my mother was arranging the places she asked my father whether he should take in the wife of a General, a difficult Madame Sans Gêne, or a peer's daughter, married to a Staff Colonel. Knowing that India had an official precedence rather than a social one, they decided to plump for the General's wife.

The moment the party ended and the guests left, my mother exclaimed : " What a mistake we've made ! " " What do you mean ? ", said my father, " I noticed nothing ! ". " My dear, it was awful," said my mother, " surely you noticed their faces ? ". My father, of course, delivered his famous address on her imagination and she snatched up her candlestick and sailed majestically to bed. The following day a peon, like the Footman in "Alice in Wonderland", arrived with a letter. It was from the Colonel. It ran " Dear Parsons, You have been such a short time in India that it is natural that you should not have yet mastered Indian precedence. Actually a peer's daughter ranks before the wife of a Major-General. Yours etc." My father took a half sheet of His Majesty's paper. " Dear S. Thank you for your letter. I much regret the inconvenience my mistake must have caused you. Yours sincerely,". He found that this protocol was mercifully supported by a numbered list, so future trouble could be averted.

Our staff was large and efficient and appeared able to cope with the " pigeon " Hindustani, which we slowly acquired.

SNATCHED UP HER CANDLESTICK AND SAILED MAJESTICALLY TO BED.

My two years in India completed my official apprenticeship in loyalist training. It could hardly have been better staged ; Simla, the Calcutta State Ball to honour the Prince and Princess of Wales, later King George V and Queen Mary, winters in the Punjab, Kashmir, and a Christmas in a Rajput Maharajah's Palace, with carriage and six.

Our winters were based in the British Cavalry lines at Ambala while my father made his rounds of inspection. From there my mother and I did our daily routine rides to exercise the horses and I played tennis at the inevitable

Club. Shortly after my arrival my mother handed over
the housekeeping to me when her little Welsh maid who
had hitherto run the *ménage* got married. Every morning
pen in hand I sat waiting for the bills. The Kitmagar —
butler—produced his book and I put down item by item
the purchases of the previous day at the Bazaar. I suppose
we were cheated more or less correctly ! I was fond of
the Kitmagar and it must have been reciprocated as on
the night of our earthquake he summoned me out on to
the verandah before anyone else. It was a very nasty
shock, although we were miles away from its centre, at
Dramsala, and the recurrent tremors made one curiously
sea-sick. Lady Sclater of Woolwich days was staying at
the time and we all collected outside the verandah com-
paring notes and reciting experiences.

My parents could not have been less colour conscious,
my father in practice and my mother in principle. She
had the strongest views on behaviour to natives, though
in actual fact colour affected her so much that she disliked
even being touched by a native. I think I was half way
between them until I noticed our Ayah's nice little girl
Tara. Tara, who was about ten years old, became my
slave and I was devoted to her. She fielded my tennis
balls and I took her everywhere with me, dressed in smart
scarlet coat and white sari. Finally, when we went to
Goulmerg in Kashmir and the famous golf club, she became my caddy. Here she bossed it over every boy caddy
on the course. Woe ! to any one of them who pinched
my balls. She would eagerly await the uncertain course
of my wooden shots and pounce on my ball where it lay.
On a fatal day I decided that she should do my swearing
for me, and when I bluffed my drive, I would look at her
and Tara, inexpressively coy, shyly obliged " dem, dem,
dem ". Naturally I felt appropriately relieved but the

co-operation became too well known and the growing crowd that followed us round embarrassed Tara so much that it was unkind to persist.

I was only seventeen when I arrived in India and the excitement of rejoining my parents, of coming out and seeing a new country upset any composure I might have had. Curiously enough much of my enjoyment was spoilt by a childish fear of being bitten by a snake and of getting enteric. I think I was a bit of a prig and did not fit comfortably into the social rhythm, while I was too young to profit by the fuller experience. Also I had been brought up to believe that if you were a " lady " you were very easily shocked. Such a definition of " U " to-day is too comical to be credible.

Things, if not quite as Kipling has told of Simla, still reflected a strong Hill complex for wives in the cool and men in the plains.

Next to Viceregal Lodge and Snowden of Lord Kitchener, the Simla Dramatic Club, which ran its own theatre and barred all professional shows, was the focus of the Season. The well-to-do rented boxes and the floor was sometimes let out for dances and cotillons to the *élite*. I need not say that I was not for a moment permitted to take part in a play there. My disappointment over this was more than compensated when Lady Amptill invited me to take part in " She stoops to Conquer " at Viceregal Lodge. To be in a company, properly produced, where people had to know their lines and not miss rehearsals, was good enough ; to have an audience which was commanded to attend was even better.

The Amptills were charming people, much more popular than the Curzons, for whom they deputised that Season.

As the Season progressed I grew less awkward and began to make friends.

There was always tennis — and the dances. Also a cricket match, mixed and very smart, where I made 36. I was never allowed to ride alone with a young man, or " to make myself conspicuous ". It seems fantastic to this generation, but until my husband and I were engaged, we never used Christian names.

My first Simla Season was somewhat dimmed by the ascetic bachelor influence of Lord Kitchener, who discouraged young officers from coming up to the social whirl. Ambitious for their future, they grew beards and went off, disguised as " *jungle-Wallahs* ", on dangerous expeditions.

The Chief was a queer man, enthralled by a passion for collecting *objets d'art*. His devoted personal staff ministered to this obsession and Colonel Fitzgerald, who perished with him in the " Hampshire ", told me that they had managed very well after the Boer War in getting the large English cities to give him silver and even gold plate instead of the usual caskets containing " Freedoms ". He mentioned that one of them complained that it was a bit expensive ; but if the City Fathers sighed they politely complied. At that dinner party we small fry ate off silver, but at a central table the twelve seniors dined entirely off gold. During dinner a gorgeous servant whispered something to Fitzgerald sitting next to me. With a hasty apology Fitzgerald hurried off and returned with a pattern of green brocade. "He's been waiting for it all day " he said and took it to the Chief's Table. It was to cover a wall panel. Not a tin tack went in without his consent. It is a fact that soldiers who followed his lead in attending auctions would hide their purchases from his covetous eye. My father was in a friend's office when word came that the Chief was expected. The occupier ran round the room clasping a recently purchased vase to his bosom and just in time popped it into the waste paper basket under a memorandum.

All this is at a tangent but I will draw nearer to the point in recalling Lord Kitchener's assertion made to my mother, that he was much more Irish than Roberts, " that's why I understand them." Actually his family came from East Anglia but he spent some years in Ireland. We shall see later how this delusion was to influence his judgment.

The social climax of the Royal Tour was the Calcutta State Ball for which Lady Sclater kindly invited me. One thought nothing of a three day train journey and to stay in such safe company I was allowed to accept. It was a wonderful week with dinner parties and a trip up the Howghli for a French lunch at Pont de Shey where one ate the sort of omelette only born in France. The Royal visit coincided with the official mission of two important Lamas from Tibet. I don't know whether I remember them correctly but I believe one was the Tashi Lama. I know I lined up with other excited onlookers to watch their short processional arrival through the streets. We were all excited to see these strange mystical personalities from their obscure holy city of Lhassa. The cars passed us slowly and the two figures in their fusty clothes, which are never removed till they fall off and new ones put on top, looked as gay and as excited as we were. Then " it " overpowered us, actually overpowered us, although clearly the cars must have been several feet distant. Years of *ghi*, butter, smoke, and what my mother called *esprit de corps* was too much for the ageing garments and the smell was something never to be equalled. We reeled away, I feel I can smell it still.

During the afternoon of the enormous garden party a private tent had been prepared for their Royal Highnesses's tea. The sight of this special peep show was too much for the Lamas and in they pressed to see what was inside. No protest could hold them back and they were only led away as the special guests precessed in for their tea. They did not partake. One sniff was enough and even the conscientious George and the resolute Mary hastily left for the open air.

The State Ball was, of course, everything that a State Ball could be in India and I remember the truly wonderful Princess in glittering white as she danced with a tall English officer of the Indian Cavalry, turban, long spurred boots and white breeches.

Looking back on these two years, I do not recall places as much as the people I met. Among them was Colonel Birdwood, subsequently the Field Marshal, and from South African days an intimate of my father's. They were a delightful family. "Birdie" used to call to me : "Come here I've remembered a story for you ". It might have been about the City Imperial Volunteer leading his horse on the veldt. Birdie, on the second day, asked why he was not riding ; had the horse a bad back ? "Broke me stirrup leather, Sir ". "Why does that stop you ? " "Left leather, Sir," "But what the devil — ? " "Can't mount, Sir." "Use the right leather, can't you ? " "Why I'd be ficing the wrong wiy." And Birdie and I would really enjoy it.

The other Field Marshal to be was Douglas Haig, a quiet, still, exclusive person, the Cavalry opposite in Command to my father. I should imagine he was the complete antithesis in every way to Lord Montgomery of the generation after him, who, naturally, I never met.

During my two years in India I saw nothing but British

cantonment life and caught only rare glimpses of the men and women who lived as civilians or in the Indian Army, in close and helpful personal contact with Indians. It is all over now, pleasures and pains, sport and bad climates, lots of servants, sand, and queer illnesses ; and always the unbearable separations between parents and their children.

What now remains of the Courts where Britons gloried and drank deep, of the red and gold servants, the state elephants and the bevy of visiting memsahibs ? Nothing. What are left are the people whom none of us bothered to notice — much — the Christian missionaries of all denominations.

How ridiculous we thought them then in their unfashionable solar topees and how gullible in making " bad Christians instead of good heathen ". These people may have attracted the respect of Indians by their schools, hospitals and zenana work but they kept it because they upheld the Christian ideal of individual significance. Even in England, later,I remember the excitement some time in the twenties, when the young missionary doctor, Mrs. Starr, went alone to the N.W. Frontier and brought back the kidnapped Ellis girl. The whole army in India could only tremble for her and stand still.

Away on shikar at Kashmir in '06 we had the pleasant news that my father was to command the 6th Division in Ireland. Strange to say, except for little Tara I left India without a single regret.

We were given a farewell party at the Bombay Yacht Club, strictest social preserve of the white ruling class, and sat enjoying the lovely evening where from across the weedless English lawn one could watch the lighted liner awaiting its complement next day. It was taking home mothers to join their children and leave their husbands, or couples facing retirement after a lifetime unfitting them for " home ". If the brightest jewel in the British Crown brought treasure and glory to Britain, it was paid for in the lives of its Crown servants.

ACROSS THE WEEDLESS ENGLISH LAWN ONE COULD WATCH THE LIGHTED LINER AWAITING ITS COMPLEMENT NEXT DAY.

CHAPTER VIII

GOVERNMENT HOUSE.

Our next official appearance in Ireland was in Government House, Cork a large and needlessly ugly villa on a hill-top, flanked by a screen wall, topped with bogus battlements. There was a flagstaff in front.

We were warned, as a General Commanding, my father represented the power if not the person of the Crown and was more important than he would have been in the same rank in England. Much impressed, my mother bought a poodle.

We arrived just before the hunting season opened and my parents busily concerned themselves collecting some mounts, two of which could also draw the official carriage. The dual purpose steeds had breeding and showed it when driving on the steep hill upon which Government House was perched. There came the day when Lady Aberdeen visited the city and, buttressed by two Bishops and every doctor in Co. Cork, addressed a meeting on Tuberculosis. It lasted two hours over time on a cold day. Apart from her own frozen feet, my mother became apprehensive. Our carriage was waiting outside to convey Her Excellency to luncheon. Their career up the cork-screw hill was even more staccato than she had feared. As her large and stately guest grew paler, my mother felt that her beloved horses must be excused. " You see, Your Excellency, they are on *extra oats*. They are to be hunted to-morrow." The stately guest paled still further.

Although she had only one horse, it became an accepted

fact that my mother hated staying away — " too busy hunting," people would explain, — but my father was often the Aberdeens' guest in Dublin and he had a regard and liking for this public spirited couple who, as Crown liberals, satisfied neither side in the existing political tension. It was their personal award for the competition on a Dublin Town Plan, before the first War, that was won by Professor Abercrombie and Mr. Sydney Kelly. The survey then made, and many of the proposals in it, formed the basis for the subsequent Draft Report drawn up by the same consultants in 1939. My husband had then been co-opted as joint consultant on the work and always appreciated what the city owed to the enthusiasm and unselfishness of the two Aberdeens, who had been mocked and belittled to an unbelievable extent by the conservative anti-liberal element in Ireland.

Other wives of Lords Lieutenant left impressions on the country that have outclassed political rancour : Lady Dudley's personal hard work for District Nursing helped to fill in distressing gaps. The associations established had so high a reputation with doctors that they have been kept up and have added to their usefulness.

Returning to Cork : I did not share my mother's passion for the chase. Frankly I was scared stiff of horses. Only moral cowardice got me to a meet, that and perhaps reaction to the subtle suggestion that with my long back, in an expensive habit, " you look your best on a horse ". Recollections of ten miles swaying on an Irish outside car on a cold day, with blue funk ahead, remain a tribute to what the strong-minded can do to the weak. In principle my mother disliked hounds and liked foxes but she looked at neither in her pleasure at galloping and jumping. My father loved watching hounds work, and always followed his own line, but he had not her love for unnecessary jumping and lacked the edge of her enthusiasm on a bad day. " Fields " were enormous with the " United " and sport was the apex of garrison and Unionist life.

Rear-Admiral Craddock, then on a half-pay spell, rode with a passionate gusto, foreshadowing Coronel, an incident of world concern that was surely not a defeat so much as victory for courage and audacity. A good number of farmers came out but I doubt whether love of foxhunting is as widespread among the Irish generally as devotees make out. With a few, yes, but, compared with the public enthusiasm for point-to-point races, it comes a bad second. The motor car as an adjunct to hunting was then only beginning and motor vanning of horses was unknown. It was hard work and jog, jog, from cover to cover and, although I remember one or two hunts which I really enjoyed, I kept the resolution which I had made to my mother and, from the day I married, I never mounted a horse again.

Because she disliked seeing anything shot, and could not bear the cold of the big Irish uncentrally-heated houses, my mother never attended shooting parties and I went in her place. These were the spot-light functions of the highest life. For the givers they were expensive hobbies, even apart from game preservation ; at least six guns, their ladies, and attendant servitors made up the visiting party. One arrived after tea on the evening before and changed. One's minimum trousseau involved three Ascot and three full evening frocks. Generally everyone wore their " black " on the second night, so it was more discerning to hold it over for the last evening. As an unmarried girl I need not have a " black," but I had to have my own maid. The first time I stayed away, my mother did not send with me the French one, acquired with Alphonse, the poodle. Because of an old hunting accident, my mother had difficulty in doing her hair ; because I had been atrociously brought up, so had I. So, both in Ascot and Best Evening, I came down with my heavy locks badly camouflaging the vast pad over which they had to be trained. Moreover no one brought me hot water, early tea, or " undid me ". In such a house any woman without her maid was a displaced person, a Society Refugee. Between tea and dinner, we did elaborate embroidery or played bridge, frizzled if near the huge fire, frozen if beyond its ambit. The dinners were long but delicious, on lovely plate, accompanied by champagne. Once my hostess wrote a few words on the crested menu card and had it sent to me by the footman. I unfolded it and read :

" You don't like woodcock."

Dutifully I turned my head from its plump bosom, teed

" YOU DON'T LIKE WOODCOCK."

up on brown toast. After forty years, the incident still rankles.

At the shoot the ladies stood by the men's loaders and watched the day's sport and joined in the game-pie lunch.

AT THE SHOOT THE LADIES STOOD BY THE MEN'S LOADERS AND WATCHED THE DAY'S SPORT

On the final morning we were given birds and sent back in the brake to the station. Cars were only then beginning to accelerate the timing.

These functions followed strict formulae. The first shoots were reciprocal, only givers of same were invited to same. At second shoots, with slightly smaller bags, there were distinguished casuals, such as the General at Cork. I was found to be a convenient odd woman out because I liked listening to older men and was, therefore, often invited on my own to first shoots.

The hierarchy of Irish social order was not defined, it did not need to be, it was deeply implicit. In England the nobility were fewer and markedly more important than over here and they were seated in the mansions considered appropriate. Here, the seventy or so Union peers, created to pass the Union, had put up our proportion of noblemen and many commoners held as good a status ; the seats, though certainly large enough, were not on the English scale.

The top social rows were then too well-known and accepted to be written down but, because a new generation may be interested and amused, I will have a shot at defining an order so unreal and preposterous as to be like theatricals in fancy dress. Although breeding was essential it still had to be buttressed by money.

Row A. Peers who were Lord or Deputy Lieutenants, High Sheriffs and Knights of St. Patrick. If married adequately their entrenchment was secure and their sons joined the Guards, the 10th Hussars or the R.N.

Row B. Other peers with smaller seats, ditto baronets, solvent country gentry and young sons of Row A, (sons in Green Jackets, Highland regiments, certain cavalry, gunners and R.N.).

Row A used them for marrying their younger children.

Row C. Less solvent country gentry, who could only allow their sons about £100 a year. These joined the Irish Regiments which were cheap ; or transferred to the Indian Army. They were recognised and respected by A and B and belonged to Kildare St. Club.

Row D. Loyal professional people, gentlemen professional farmers, trade, large retail or small wholesale, they could often afford more expensive Regiments than Row C managed. Such rarely cohabited with Rows A and B but formed useful cannon-fodder at Protestant Bazaars and could, if they were really liked, achieve Kildare St.

Absurd and irritating as it may seem to-day, this social

hierarchy dominated our acceptances.

I had the benefit of always meeting a social cross section by playing a good deal of match tennis. In Cork I am glad to say I made many friends in Row D and below it. The top Rows rarely joined clubs and their play suffered. The exceptions were the Bechers of Ballygiblin, Co. Cork (Row A). Adeline, who married Willy Barry, had an undercut like the kick of a deft mule. Playing against her, one's left-hand tram line was stabbed by the round marks where her ball punched it. She beat every woman in Ireland, until Mrs. Sterry brought the volley to Fitzwilliam in Dublin. The sisters eschewed the graces ; they wore heavy blue skirts, starched collars and hard round hats, long after the rest of us had relaxed our outfits. Adeline won her club singles at 70 and, when past 80, played an attacking mixed double. She was also a magnificent rider.

There were perhaps a dozen (also very loyal) Roman Catholic families who qualified for the first two Rows ; many more, equally loyal but less distinguished, moved freely with the last two.

Amongst these " Row A " Roman Catholics were the Kenmares, living in a long, gracious house at Killarney. Like Bantry House, in an equally lovely situation, it was of brick instead of the prevailing stone of Ireland. It faced the chosen view of all that district. My father and I stayed there for an exceptionally pleasant shoot, after a heavy and rare fall of snow. Brilliant sun illuminated the familiar scenery ; in its strange guise it looked as excited and self-conscious as a bride. The principal reception rooms had door handles formed of the embossed backs of old gold watches. No one had mentioned this feature to me and it is a life-long regret that I turned them nonchalantly as though they had been brass.

In the morning, before joining the guns, we women were waiting in the very large hall ; there was brought in a most important Bishop, upholstered in purple. The cluster of Browne ladies by the fire genuflected and kissed his ring, with the lubricated expertise of born Roman Catholics and courtiers. I was writing by the window. As I eyed the slippery parquet, the nails in my sports shoes grew longer. The door, however, was further away than the fire. I hope my tribute, when accomplished, was not sufficiently clumsy to let the heretic show through.

The late Lord Castlerosse, the eldest son, was then a slender lad. He became a portly first-rate columnist and, after he succeeded his father, planned his estate for the local good. Killarney House had been accidentally burnt some time after we stayed there, and the watch-backs perished with it.

The Kildare Street Club in Dublin was the Unionist focus. It appeared then as the symbol of what was unchangeable and absolute. It dates from the end of the 18th century and was at first more social than political. During the Home Rule struggle it became wholly political but has since adjusted itself to circumstances, admits women to part of the premises, and others who would not have been welcomed in the old snob days — or might then have disliked the very thought of it. The Club, with good cooking, preserves a dignified retreat in what is a lovely casket of Victorian architecture. Who has not admired the skittish carved monkeys playing billiards round the windows ?

The County Club at Cork was even more given to blackballs than Kildare Street. The ineligibles, mostly Roman Catholic business folks, or anyone whose loyalty was suspect, joined the City Club where they claimed to enjoy the better cellar.

When we arrived in Cork the County Club was still divided between those who had sided with the Committee or with the Plaintiff, in a recent law suit connected with cards. Before we issued invitations to a party, I had to consult a list showing the personnel of the two sides. Feeling was too strong for it to be tactful to ask opposite sides to the same party.

Because of a curious corollary, I am venturing to give a brief sketch of the events. The principals are now all dead but what I have now to tell is a fact that could not have been disclosed at the time. The plaintiff was a rich young man, married to one of the most beautiful women in Ireland. They were very much taken up by Row A and this caused some jealousy in the B ranks. Moreover it cannot be disputed that he was an ungracious loser at games, which made him unpopular. Play for high stakes began at the Club and it soon became clear that something crooked was going on. Because he was unpopular and because he was winning, suspicion fell on the young man. Feeling became so assured and so strong that the Committee through its Hon. Secretary asked him to resign from the Club. He had no option but to bring an action for slander against the Committee. The case became deplorably personal. All the plaintiff's partisan friends in Row A were called as witnesses and, under cross examination, made very poor ones. It was accepted that there had been manipulation but it could not be proved exactly where it lay. The plaintiff won his verdict. The damages, however, were assessed at only one farthing.

Such a decision could not placate either side and it took many years for the bitterness to die down, but the plaintiff's family wisely weathered out the odium and stayed on in Cork.

Now for the corollary : while overseas my father had

come across a certain officer, serving in one of H.M. less fashionable oceanic stations. This man was a master at all forms of card manipulation ; finally no one at the station would play at his table ; it was perhaps for that reason that he was serving where he was. When years later we arrived in Cork, my father found out accidentally that this officer, now retired, was a member of the County Club ; he also ascertained that he had been playing during the whole period in question. No one had the least suspicion of his methods ; he was so quiet and un-assuming. My father never told me the man's name nor could he reveal the story to anyone else. All those con-cerned are, of course, dead and the particular man's place in the drama will never be known.

Dances then were not subject to fixed parties from which no member might stray. We privateered. The successful had a splendid time but the unresourceful a wretched one. The word " wall-flower " was then coined to describe their fate. The difference which smart ready-made frocks have made to the general average appear-ance is revolutionary. Either you went to a good, expensive, dress-maker or to a dud. If a dud, you looked a show ; long hair badly coiffed and no make-up finished you. The virtuous may have taken comfort that they were as their Creator made them but that was all the consolation they had, as they sat unbidden and unfed. To many the dances were funerals more than entertain-ments.

Among the big social events of those Cork days was the " United Kingdom Quadrille ", staged as a special attraction for a large Charity Ball. Smart colonels' wives of English, Scottish and Welsh regiments organised decorative national sets. The Gordons did an enchanting eight-hand reel. We Irish were mobilised by dear old

Lady Bandon and were extremely grand but unbecoming. The men were dull beside their kilted rivals and wore

WE PRIVATEERED

coats with emerald green lapels, but we luckless women were swathed in shapeless yards of ditto coloured tulle and looked deadly. I was paired with my distant St. Leger kinsman, the late Lord Doneraile, who, at the time, was only interested in a contraption he had invented for measuring when a ball was over the boundary line at croquet. None of us had rehearsed our steps and we floundered about, the acknowledged flop of the evening. Perhaps we were only typical of what happened when the Anglos of that day tried to become " all out Irish ". During the years I spent in Cork, I never met a Nationalist and only about three English liberals.

At that time some very smart Cavalry regiments were stationed at Ballincollig, near Cork, and their exciting marriages to popular musical comediennes was one of our topics as the unions waxed or waned. At one time they kept and hunted a " bobbery " pack of hounds. The Master of these told me of the rebuffed farmer who had had his hay cast as unfit for the Hunt horses. He was furious. " But," said my friend the Master, " you know it was bad hay." " It was so ", said the farmer ; " It's not that that's annoying me, but the young gentleman that cast it belonged to that accursed race that killed our Blessed Saviour."

No personal recollection is more absorbing to me than the day when Baden Powell, while having tea with us, told my mother and me of the new movement for boys which he, largely encouraged by Seton Thomson, was about to start. He was a truly inspiring individual and I had on order the first book on Scouting long before it came out. Disastrously, I lost it. B. P. was typical of the Cavalry officer who was too melodramatic, too sensational, to be popular with his fellows. He was suspected of Propaganda. Yet it was probably his qualities of showmanship which helped to put his idea across and change the lives of so many young people. My children, as truculent individualists, all failed to respond to the whistle, though one or two, to please me, made a faint effort. I am glad to say that some of my grandchildren seem to have reverted to type !

Then there was the Fleet which frequently invaded Bantry Bay for a noisy exercise called " Calibrating ". Every window rattled and some broke, compensation followed. Our party tossed over in a wet picket boat in our best clothes to dine with Admiral Beatty, from Co. Wexford, in the " Queen ". The cabin in which our appearances were restored looked like a film star's dressing room. This apparently was an amenity on which his rich American wife insisted. An armed quartermaster stood outside the door, while we effected repairs. We also used to dance in the battle cruisers " Invincible " and her sister ships ; which afterwards met their tragic ordeal at Jutland. The gunnery officers laid rifle tubes along the big guns for practice at small floating targets. My father was once asked to show his skill and, being quite unaccustomed to the art, gave an erratic display which rejoiced the sailors. Admiral Purefoy, a Dubliner, came down from the quarter-deck and unloosed a forceful verbal opinion of the silly boob's shooting. He was dismayed when he saw who the boob was.

He asked me if I had heard what he said and I replied that I now knew my father was a curate compared with him. When they both retired they constantly met at their club, " the Rag ", and he always called my father " the curate."

The Admiral at Queenstown, now Cobh, was dear little George King-Hall, father of Commander Stephen King-Hall. He was what my father described as " professionally good " and the latter was always afraid of shocking him. That fine sailor, Prince Louis of Battenburg, came constantly to luncheon to talk the latest gunnery ; generally we saw quite a lot of the blue water school. Once when my mother was present their conversation wandered to an offensively snobbish wife of an Admiral. " Ah ! but she wouldn't show it to you ", said my mother. He gravely replied : " The worst snobs I have known in my life were all royalty."

After King Edward died, we had to put off a full house for an amateur show at the Opera House and lose our charity over £100. At the special service at St. Finbarr's Cathedral, Lady Bandon and the *élite* eclipsed themselves in loyal grief, wearing long black veils like Italian widows. After the solemn day, I was going up for May fly " dapping " in Lough Sheelan in Co. Cavan, and therefore secured a completely new black Sunday suit so as to adapt myself to my Ulster hosts. I underdid my loyalty by not also buying black (or mottled black) tweeds for the boat. All in brown, I felt frivolous and disloyal among them. They were, I am sure, dyed black to the skin like the enthusiast who played Othello. They did wear white for tennis, but black belts, hats and stockings. It must be remembered that Co. Cavan was border Ulster, with a dangerous majority of the disloyal around them, so it was most important to show *them* what one felt.

King Edward was liked in Ireland. This sometimes took expression in wall chalkings : " The King has been to Holy Mass. He is a Roman Catholic." This idea was quite widely held. His death was the end of our ordered world. From now on the rumblings became too loud not to be heeded. There was so much of it, all disturbing. The Suffragettes were not in Ireland, but we shook our heads and read about them. Worst of all, the Liberals were in power. Home Rule was looming larger. The Crown party in the South became self-conscious and joined first-aid classes, to be ready to tend the Ulster Volunteers, who were beginning to drill. Among the more moderate, or less nervous, there was some talk of Federalism. William O'Brien's political panacea of devolution was believed bogus, just a dodge to split Redmond. Lord Dunraven's devolution had a kinder reception because it was so unlikely to be accepted. He did, however, start many people thinking. He used to stay with us in Cork and I still remember his lecture on " Moose Calling " — and felt a bit like a moose myself.

My mother, however, was now well out of official Unionist graces and detested Carson. I had been groping for guidance since I had seen W. G. Fay play in ' The Rising of the Moon " and had discovered that I had actually laughed at an R.I.C. policeman : the *lèse majesté* nearly kept me awake at night. I had also read " The Seething Pot " and seethed in sympathy. This may have been a trivial and amateur reaction, but then emotions often are like that ; quite a few young people were at that time in the mood described by Bermingham in his earlier books, before he retired to England and lived happily ever afterwards. None of us could decide what we wanted : could there be no compromise ?

Compromise was the last thing that either extreme Nationalists or ultra-Unionists desired. Crown loyalty had never been stronger, except that the wearer of the Crown, King George V, was himself an uncertain factor. Many agreed with the Ulsterman who complained, " the King is no good. He's not loyal."

It is easy now to criticize the Unionists of those days ; we forget that at that time the mystique of Nationality had not been generally formulated and to the generation brought up as we had been under British responsibility the risk of embarking on independence appeared disastrous and likely to injure not only Unionists but the whole country. Moreover hardly any of the Unionists were aware that there were many men of character and education on the Nationalist side. The abuse and propaganda hurled at us was as dishonest as it was unnerving and even the few Anglo-Irish who had read a word of Irish history believed that past wrongs were no argument for revolutionary experiment. With the Conservative Party solidly behind us and with Ulster and her massed Volunteers drilling for resistance, it was natural for the Anglo-Irish element in the South to believe that if only we held firm we might avoid being " betrayed " by the Liberals.

CHAPTER IX

MR. AND MRS. SHAW IN IRELAND.

Bernard Shaw's connection with Ireland influenced his life to a greater extent than is generally realised. It is common knowledge that he was born at 33, Synge Street, Dublin, in 1856. It is less well known that he lived in the Dublin coastal resort of Dalkey from about 1865 until 1870, while the town quarters of the family was at 1, Hatch Street. Still less is the public aware of the close connection Shaw maintained with the " Old Ascendancy " in Ireland during the years when his reputation was already established.

It was before the first World War that I came across the Shaws. It was at the time — about 1908 — that my father was commanding the Cork district and, as a girl living in Government House, I had special opportunities of meeting the Anglo-Irish world. In England Charlotte Shaw was best known by her connection with the Webb group, but her Will, if it did nothing else, reminded English people that this quiet, highly intelligent person was a very well-off Irishwoman. In his letters to Ellen Terry, written before his marriage, Bernard nearly always alluded to Charlotte as the " millionairess " ; in his letters after his marriage — few of which are addressed to other women — the allusions reflect the comradeship they shared. The fact that Bernard gave every appearance of enjoying and not merely of submitting to the annual family holiday spent among the early associations of the Payne-Townshends, shows how deeply rooted the mutual affinity had become. If Charlotte was not born she was reared in the Big House and it takes more than the influence of the Fabian circle to change an Irishwoman fashioned by pre-1914 days. Charlotte's controversial Will is likely to have been an unexpected product of such fashioning.

To say that it was natural for Charlotte to revert to the Irish associations of her forebears is to make things too easy, since it ignores the important factor that Charlotte had an English mother, and derived her income from England. Her father, Horace Townshend (the h. in the name was added arbitrarily by him and others), married the eldest daughter of Colonel Thomas Kirby, " devisee under the Will of Thomas Payne of his estates situate at Edbaston, Salop ". On succeeding to these agreeable estates " on the right of his wife ", Horace assumed the name of Payne-Townshend. In recalling the past, especially after over thirty years, it is difficult to disentangle first-hand memories from talk heard later, but our young generation then circulating through the social life of Co. Cork was keenly interested in all that appertained to the curiously assorted quartette formed around the provocative celebrity. Local social authorities credited Charlotte and her sister with £10,000 a year each, an income not subject to the certain and familiar deflation associated with Irish landed estates. Derry, the Townshend property, had, on Horace's death, devolved upon his brother, but the estates " situate at Edbaston, Salop ", or their equivalent were shared equally between Charlotte and her younger sister, Mary. Only faint astonishment was expressed by the neighbours when Charlotte — known to her contemporaries as " Miss Plain Townshend " — apparently decided to eschew men and adopt socialism in London. It was considered to be even less astonishing that the equally well dowered but more comely Mary should marry the appropriate Hugh

Cholmondeley of the Rifle Brigade, nephew of Lord Delamere.

Colonel Cholmondeley, when I first saw him, was middle-aged and unusually good-looking. Tall, blue-eyed with crinkled fair hair, his appearance fascinated the citizens of London when, after the South African war, he rode through their thronged streets leading the City Imperial Volunteers. He was of the inner circle of Cheshire, which, screened by the closeringed Tarporley Hunt Club, strove to keep itself unspotted from the world of Manchester. Travelling around in his graceful worn tweeds, he conveyed the perfection of a long Georgian spoon — " bright-cut " — like his eyes and hair. I can still remember how deeply I envied the friend to whom he sympathetically presented a copy of Kipling's verse.

Charlotte had married later than Mary and we girls liked to believe, I know erroneously, that she and Bernard had been too high-minded to submit to bourgeois wedlock but had lived in sinful virtue in a tenement, with a geranium on the window-sill. Anyhow the sisters were deeply attached to each other and the disparity of outlook between the husbands that kept them for some time apart made them both miserable. Fortunately the husbands were affectionate spouses and sensible men and an annual *vacance carrée* was instituted. Later it strayed abroad, but until 1914, it prevailed in the Co. Cork of the Payne-Townshends, spreading to hotels at Glengariff and Park-nasilla. I do not think that Bernard found the visits to country houses as uncongenial as his admirers might wish to imagine. No pubs for him. He was not himself reared in the Big House but he was only a generation removed from it, a generation into which Protestant professional classes entered. Some of these relations have told me of his generosity (anonymous) even to his distant kinsmen,

and I also know that some years before his death he was
in most friendly correspondence with his cousins of Bushey
Park, Dublin, and with the young son of the present
baronet, Sir Robert Shaw. True, it amused him to de-
precate his immediate relations and to annoy them by
belittling the Shaw family, but would it have been Shaw
if he hadn't ? In a letter to my husband concerning the
Dun Laoghaire — then Kingstown — neighbourhood
where his boyhood was spent he alludes to the privilege
of access to Dalkey Hill, which was acquired through
" written orders of admission to the local gentry in virtue
of which I had the run of the hill ".

Bernard lacked all snobbery, including that which dis-
likes its own class, but he definitely enjoyed observing
that class from outside and I have not heard that he
expressed any particular impatience with the circle he
visited during those years. You could see that Charlotte
did not need to observe her hosts and their friends ; she
was of them and, although she might prefer to live away
and serve other ideals, once a year regularly she would
come back with Mary and Hugh to sink again into the
life of her own kind.

Invariably the party visited Mitchelstown Castle, in
Co. Cork, then owned by my mother's old cousin, Anna,
Lady Kingston. Turretted and battlemented, the building covered a greater area than did any other private
house in Ireland. It had a superb spread, a dramatic
sky-line and, — however bogus the castellations — the
hand-craft of its masonry lifted it into the ranks of
architecture. I shall not forget the dignity of its mutilated
line, backed by the Galtee mountains, after its destruction
in the Troubles. It was a sinister and melancholy sil-
houette to those of us, in my case from infancy, who had
enjoyed its hospitality.

Mitchelstown had never been a lucky house. The Lord Kingston of the day had " restored ' it, in place of an older castle, in order to provide a truly impressive welcome to King George IV, who had promised to stay with him when he visited Ireland. The King visited Ireland but he left out Mitchelstown. Later, riots, boycotts and law-suits had dogged the family and the castle devolved upon Anna, widow of the 6th earl. She devoted

INVARIABLY THE PARTY VISITED MITCHELSTOWN CASTLE.

her long life to the quiet re-establishment of the property, and the part of the house which she occupied was maintained in the most perfect taste. She died before its destruction and the heavy compensation awarded by an uncomfortable British Government was expended by her successor upon a commercial building scheme elsewhere.

Despite disparity of age, there was an abiding friendship between Anna and Charlotte, who was not the first woman reformer to have stayed at Mitchelstown. In

1787 a more colourful revolutionary had been engaged as governess by Lady Kingsborough. In her letters, Mary Woolstonecraft complained with bitterness of the " solemn stupidity " of the older castle. There was nothing solemn or stupid about Anna or her surroundings and, even during his most provocative years, " Mr. Shaw ", so my cousin would assure me, " is always most pleasant to me." While Charlotte exuded political intellectuality, Anna was passive and conservative ; both revered the beautiful, Charlotte rather consciously, while with Anna the attitude was more a life-long deference than a passion. I recollect her composed qualification for the best Nanking porcelain ; " The white ", she pointed out, " must be the white of a young eye ". If Anna was dignified rather than dynamic, her family made up for the deficiency ; her brother, Captain Richard Brinkley, representing " The Times ", became the outstanding authority upon Japan and — consecutively — married two Japanese ladies. Her cousins included the Clan Graves and among her great-nephews is Mr. Cyril Connolly.

The most important bedroom in the Castle was " The King's ". On the only occasion when I had the privilege to occupy it, my husband and I counted 41 stairs to get to the 1st floor. The room was square and of such a size that on a misty night it was difficult to see across it. I have a recollection of a deep crimson flock wall paper with a velvety pile that had resisted deterioration for upwards of a century. The immense canopied four-poster was like a fortress, only gained by assault, crowning, as it did, the summit of a raised platform. Nothing less than this royal apartment was considered suitable for dear Charlotte and the pleasant Mr. Shaw. I like to imagine his then carroty beard jutting out of the sheets beneath the crimson canopy. Perhaps the distraction of it all accounted for his leaving his pyjamas behind him. I know I arrived at the castle the day after the Shaw party had left to find the household disturbed but flattered by his lengthy telegram in which he deplored how " the celebrated author had left pyjamas, camera, etc.".

Anna's second husband, Willie Webber, was a picturesque old man ; an all-Jaeger addict he considered it immoral to sleep in any but woollen sheets. His smallest habits were a ritual. After dinner, the butler would bring in a silver salver, upon which rested a finely chased spirit lamp, some straw spills in a stand and a snuff-box of tobacco. A filigree-covered pipe, the size of an acorn, was slowly filled with very fine golden tobacco. After lighting first a spill and then the pipe, Mr. Webber reverently executed three puffs and the whole complicated outfit was gently removed from sight. Even his anti-smoking guest must have appreciated the perfect timing of the ceremony.

Then followed some classical trios in the ante-room. An elderly cousin played the violin, Mr. Webber — with his feet fortified by immense Jaeger house-boots — the 'cello, and any guest competent to do so (my husband took the rôle during our stay) played the piano. Bernard Shaw was never more welcome at any house than he was at Mitchelstown. Unflaggingly he would support his two enthusiastic elders at the piano, being far more appreciative of their musical ardour than critical of their defects in execution.

Anna and Charlotte, sitting together, enjoyed the evenings to themselves. The annual routine was not broken until after Anna's death before the first World War.

It is a feature of Irish country house visiting — to

UNFLAGGINGLY HE WOULD SUPPORT HIS TWO ENTHUSIASTIC
ELDERS AT THE PIANO

which Elizabeth Bowen has done justice — that guests continually " just miss each other " ; and I had " just missed " the Shaw-Cholmondeleys, for several consecutive years until, in about 1911, we all converged at Bantry House, then belonging to Edward Leigh-White. This mansion, standing by the edge of Bantry Bay, contains what amounts to the Wallace Collection. The original owner, the first Lord Bantry, had been in Paris immediately after the Revolution and had taken the neat opportunity to embellish the house he was enlarging, and so do justice to his new earldom. Loot from the Tuileries was purchased for a few francs. Two of Marie Antoinette's marble mantel-pieces, an amount of Palace furniture, so many gentlemen's watches that they had to be used up to form the border for a table, and, above all, acres of Aubusson carpets and superb tapestries were shipped to the desolate edge of South-West Ireland. Crusts and cake were brought together.

That year, a week or two before the Shaws arrived, Sir Douglas Dawson had been of our party. As Lord Chamberlain, he then had charge of the King's tapestries, so the Bantry collection had a special interest for him. Other and more versatile qualities are, however, required of the holder of the office which keeps its vigilance over the morals of the King and of his subjects. The Lord Chamberlain had the final responsibility for the censorship of plays. Recently he had prohibited the public performance of " The Shewing-up of Blanco Posnet ". Sir Douglas had evidently not shifted the onus of the act on to subordinate shoulders for he was still agog with the excitement of the correspondence. He had hardly arrived before he told us of how Shaw wrote this, and he wrote that, up to the final Shaw letter. He looked every inch the Lord Chamberlain when he declared :

" I did not bother to answer the fella."

When Bernard and Charlotte arrived they " just missed " Dawson, but they were still as much excited by the prohibition as he had been. Again we were told how I wrote this, and he wrote that, until the author's last letter was recited. After repeating it Shaw gave a gusty laugh :

" Of course the man had not another word he could say ! "

At the time, I was an ardent " Shavian " prepared for quotable sensations. Alas ! my recollection of that visit is clear but disappointing. Mine was only a youthful, crude summary but I give it as sincere, though shocking. I thought I had never heard anyone talk so much and so uncritically ! He retailed long and rather trite accounts of the day when he " did " music for the weekly press. He evidently enjoyed his status as a celebrity and was highly entertained by the gaucherie of a local hotel-keeper, who had been told that the person he had been receiving unawares was *Bernard Shaw.*

" The hotel-keeper ", he said, " only remarked, ' Who *is* Bernard Shaw ? ' "

Looking back, it now seems to me that our Author had been generous to spread himself for two hours before a young girl and his quiet, unassuming host, both too shy to supply grist to the conversational mill. Perhaps this natural overflow reflected the abundance in Shaw's work, where brass is often mixed amongst the gold. He did, however, mention two memorable incidents : that he had drawn 'Enery Straker entirely from imagination but that, shortly afterwards, he had engaged a chauffeur who filled the role in every detail of phrase and character. He also described how much he had been mystified concerning the identity of the unknown benefactor behind the repertory movement then producing his plays. One night he dreamt he was looking up a long corridor with steps at the end ; suddenly he realised that walking towards him down the steps was Miss Horniman. From the moment he awoke he realised who the benefactress was.

Concerning Charlotte : she talked much less than he did but, I thought, with far greater pungency. Her competence was impressive and I cheerfully decided that it was obvious " the wife had the better brains ". One of the house party — she who had been given the enviable volume of Kipling — asked me in an undertone whether I had noticed Charlotte's clothes. I said frankly that I had not.

" That ", said my friend, " is her tragedy. Nobody ever does."

I looked once more at the rather dumpy figure, the dull, pale, bespectacled face, " Miss Plain Townshend " indeed, and then I perceived that her discreet toilette was exquisitely appropriate for an uncertain summer's day at Bantry.

" But that quiet coat and skirt is lovely ! ", I whispered.

" Never less than eighteen guineas ", (those were pre-War days) said my hard-up, practical friend ; " She is obsessed with clothes and spends lavishly."

We both stared as hard as tact would allow.

" What a waste ! "

By unkind contrast anything looked well on Mary, who seemed to be peacefully unconcerned by her own appearance. Mary was the Intelligent Woman of the Guide to Socialism.

I can still see the last flash of the scene as we stood on the steps when the Shaw car took the party away. Edward Leigh-White turned back into the house and summarised the visit.

" Nice intelligent man ! "

Before quitting Bantry it is satisfactory to tell that largely thanks to the tact and character of its owners, it did not perish as did Mitchelstown and so many other comely houses.

The two married couples continued their annual rounds, Charlotte and Mary happy in their old haunts, whilst the two affectionate husbands viewed each other across the table in silent, tolerant perplexity. As Shaw has said of another incident, the contrast was " too true to be good ". Hugh's ancient Saville Row suit and faded O.E. tie : Bernard's shapeless oatmeal coat and knicker-bockers. All four lived to be old people : two of them on mixed drink and diet; two as teetotal vegetarians.

Bernard's vigorous activities in his eighties, and after, are known to the wide world. I think, however, that, within his own scope, Hugh, the first to be widowed, maintained an equal virtuosity. At eighty, and still crinkle-haired, he married again, and this time he fathered a son.

To confirm the influence which his youthful memories of Ireland had on Shaw, I cannot do better than quote his own letter, written to my husband in February 1943 :

" I grew from ten to fourteen on Torca Hill : and the scenery — Killiney Bay to Bray Head and the Wicklow mountains from the front of the house, and Dublin Bay from Dalkey Island to Howth Head from the back garden — made a deep impression on me. I am very susceptible that way, and I count it as a factor of the first importance in my real education, which was essentially aesthetic."

CHAPTER X

UNEASY YEARS.

When my father's Command at Cork came to its normal end, he passed from half-pay to retirement and my garrison life was over, even before the War altered our world. My daughter used to twit me, when she grew up, in an age of shortages, that the lovely time I should have enjoyed was wasted on me because I was too much engrossed by other interests to be wholly absorbed by the parties ; still I think I enjoyed the lot. I had, however, begun to make friends in a wider world of ideas and books and was meeting a type of civilian with interests other than sport and games. Probably it was due to my own limitations that my new anvil did not strike sparks from the average subaltern. I told my mother, who admired their straight backs, that I hoped I would not marry a soldier. But were the nice young soldiers of those days so conventionally limited and how much does the increased know-how of to-day add to ability ? Wise men tell us not at all.

In the new world beyond the garrison horizon unexpected experiences would spring up. On a round of calls my then hostess suddenly asked me if I would like to meet Alice Meynell, the poetess, who was staying with her sister, the artist Lady Butler, in her little house by the Tipperary mountains. To this generation, Lady Butler's pictures are indeed the work of yester-year, of the Crimea that inspired them — not old enough to be classic yet hopelessly demodés. Lady Butler was more than an artist, she was an acute observer and her husband, Sir William, was considered one of the ablest Anglo-Irish

generals in the Army. She was used to meeting people
of independent ideas and came from a brilliant English
Roman Catholic family. Naturally, I accepted the offer
and we made the necessary detour and were warmly welcomed by the sisters. At that time Sir William had a
Command at Cape Town. I imagine that there must be
few young people to-day who have even heard of Lady
Butler and her work ; yet, at that time, both were household words and, owing to their suitability for repro-
duction, her Crimean soldier subjects fell from every
Christmas number, as emotional in appeal as they were
precise in detail. I know we eagerly collected any we
could pick up and framed them to adorn our plain walls
in the Fermoy Barracks. " The Roll Call " was brilliant
in technique and historically accurate to a button. It was
much her best known work but my young heart bled for
the lonely owner standing, pistol in hand, prepared to
shoot his horse as it lay in the snow : " Cruel only to
be kind." One may blush now at so monstrous an assault
on the feelings but, whether it is ranked as art or not, I
believe the sincerity of her observation will live as de-
scriptive history and as a valuable record of what it
portrayed and of what appealed to those of its day. Alice
Meynell's personality, largely owing to her connection
with Francis Thompson, is still alive in the poetic world.
Both sisters were then elderly, unconventional, with un-
tidy clothes and completely natural as they looked at one
alertly with their large dark eyes. Meeting them was
one of those events it is not trite to call a privilege.

Returning to the Garrison world, time has emphasized
how much the integration between the English garrison
and the local civilians, Anglo-Irish and native Irish,
affected both sides in the coming political balance.

The new English Pale was not a barrier erected to keep

people out, it had become the most welcoming and impressive feature of Social life. Those of us who remember the warmth and extent of that personal fellowship feel that we can understand its continued echoes which largely led to the unexplained volunteering to join the British army in World War II.

Some sixty years of social intermingling between garrison and Irish had been warmed by economic perquisites and sunned by society glamour ; it became difficult to identify the rumblings underneath. The story was still told of the fat mamma at the regimental ball : " Maria, spring to the Captain ! " This might well be taken as the slogan of the times. Maria's springs were an outrage to her Patriot brother ; the situation, agreeable as it was to Maria and to the many tradesmen who fattened on the prosperity that went with it, was anathema to the ruthless, grim young men who were to lead in the coming revolution.

Because the relationship was superimposed on an unreal situation, it became progressively harmful and provoked more hostility than it allayed. The Anglo-Irish could not recognise that, deep down, the normal native Irishman of the 19th century was obsessed by his longing for national freedom and ownership of his land. However much he might have liked the English soldier personally, he still loathed the imposition of the Crown on his Harp ; thus, while he maintained friendly social relations, and made all he could commercially from the connection, politically he worked and harangued against the presence of the garrison. Moreover, the fact that the soldiers could always be used in case of serious trouble was as annoying to the Home Ruler as it was beautiful and fortifying to the Loyalist. Neither the English officer nor the local Protestant ever fathomed the depths of the national sentiment. "They would be quite all right if they could be left alone", "It's all due to Agitation", were repeated glibly as ultimate truth. A nice old boatman at Killarney would unbosom himself

A NICE OLD BOATMAN AT KILLARNEY WOULD UNBOSOM HIMSELF
TO MY FATHER

to my father, and he would return to his realistic wife full of the hidden feelings exposed by this delightful and representative old man. How he mocked his M.P. for " ating chickens at Westminister ", whispered sarcastically of his priest's arts in raising money, and who so quickly recognised a " real gentleman from one of those cocked up jackeens." The old man was not necessarily a liar. He had moods when he felt all these emotions, but his hearer failed to realise that basically he was like every other Irishman living in Ireland, pledged eternally to his native loyalties.

The Anglo-Irish country gentlemen of my day took
their colour absolutely from the garrison, not only the
patriotic orientation of the latter but their social and
mental angle. It had become obligatory to look and speak
like an English public school man and, therefore, anyone
who could scrape together the necessary cash sent his
son to an English public school. Even if he could not afford
a renowned one yet anything was better than Ireland.
The one Southern Irish public school, St. Columba's
College at Rathfarnham, sister school to Radley, at first
seemed a reasonable and cheaper substitute but, with
the advent of quick railway travel, those who had the
money preferred the certainty of their sons getting rid
of an Irish brogue and meeting people who might be more
useful afterwards. Trinity ceased to be the right thing
for the larger county families. It was considered provin-
cial. Moreover since, as we have reluctantly observed,
it was essential for anyone with a place to keep up to
marry money, a young man educated at an expensive
English public school and a good college at Oxford or
Cambridge was more likely to meet eligible sisters. After
all, people truly believed that they were doing the best
for their sons and, the world being as it is, they probably
were.

Better off Anglo-Irishmen were less University-minded
than their contemporaries in England. Most younger
sons, and eldest sons until they inherited their patrimony,
joined the fighting services. The less well off and the professional classes still went to Trinity and supplied the
intellectual element both here and overseas. For this
reason the heads of the leading Protestant County families
were, generally speaking, less intellectually minded than
their grandfathers had been. In the country house
libraries the best books are the old ones, but go into the

hall of any Irish country house ; its walls are not only spotted with foxes' heads, pad and brushes (this would also apply to England) but, from cornice to dado, trophies from distant lands are festooned, while skins lie in wait as traps on the slippery floors.   Every young man who served in the army — and nearly every young Anglo-Irishman has — sent back to the family seat his black buck, ibex, bull bison and all.   His uncle's umbrellas are grouped in an elephant's foot.   His aunt's tea would be brought in on a Benares tray.   Even I, as a Miss Sahib in India, shot my crocodile and its head now hangs menacingly in our front hall.

Intrinsically there is no reason why active soldiers should not be as well educated and objectively minded as civilians with a University training.   But are they ? Does life in Cantonment India or in an officers' mess make for a speculative critical mind ?   Pleasant as the pre-First War soldier was, he was community trained.   He was not expected or encouraged to be original and know better than his company commander.   As intellectual outlets he was allowed to be very good at languages, geography, natural history and Bridge, but anything that was not strictly conventional in politics or sociology was suspect.   I well remember my excitement when I first met a Liberal.   Later I was to meet an Irish Liberal, Lord Castletown (" poor old Barneybalmy of course ").   Everyone agreed that it was inexplicable that such as he " should encourage class warfare ".   In England Liberals might have been uncomfortable, but they were found in the highest circles and young men at the Universities were accustomed to views contradictory to their own.   Before 1914 in Ireland, or in garrison life, one might say that some military service in India took the place of a University in Irish county family life.   These families

ITS WALLS ARE NOT ONLY SPOTTED WITH FOXES' HEADS, PAD AND
BRUSHES BUT, FROM CORNICE TO DADO, TROPHIES FROM DISTANT
LANDS ARE FESTOONED.

contributed outstanding names to the army, but can it be said that literature, art, science, Parliament, the Bar, the Church, the Civil and Colonial services are not more associated with Irishmen educated at Trinity ? During the early 19th century before it became the fashion for so many young men to join the services, the leading Irish families ranked much as the same class in England. Their leaders were University educated and objective in their views. Back-benchers will always be back-benchers from whatever class they come ; it is the leaders who count and, in England, many of them are to be found to-day in all Parliamentary parties and in administrative posts.

Here the natural Anglo-Irish leaders sat in the Kildare Street Club and represented their order.

Judged as a collection of rather misguided old soldiers, who had never in their lives mixed with educated nationalists, their deliberations may not now appear to have been very significant. But take the constitution of the British Army and the character of its officers in 1913. They were overwhelmingly Unionist, drawn as R.C.K. Ensor points out in his authoritative *Oxford History of England* " to a very disproportionate extent from the Anglo-Irish gentry." Most fateful of all such individuals was Sir Henry Wilson in the key position as Director of Military Operations. Wilson had the Ulster *idée fixe* and was a man who liked operating from behind the scenes. He was hand in glove with Carson and Bonar Law and, although in an official position, made it a habit to give and take official secrets from the War Office to the Ulster leaders. This sweeping statement could not be made if it were not for the published diaries which Wilson kept up regularly. In them he also naively asserts that he fostered the idea that Army officers should refuse to coerce Ulster.

On the Government side political expediency made

Asquith reluctant to admit that actually no one in England approved of physical coercion, and many people there were feeling that the Ulster Volunteer movement was itself coercive and bound to create like defiance in the South. Despite the strenuous attempts of many sincere people, including King George V, to find a peaceful solution the situation was allowed by the Government to drift, and by the protagonists to boil up and bubble.

The more it boiled the better it suited Wilson. His was a curious and complex character. Throughout those remarkable, unembarrassed outpourings during England's critical days before and during the War, he blithely describes his plans for defeating the Government he loathed but had pledged himself to serve. For Southern Ireland, from which he came (for, like Carson, he was not an Ulsterman) he piled up hate, which turned double-edged in his tragic end. There is no need to pursue the subject of the Crown Forces by analysing the complex balances that led to the Asquith Home Rule Bill, which became an Act in 1914 but was only made operative in 1920 — in the Six Counties alone. What does concern us is the army influence on Irish affairs, after Carson's volunteers had been copied by the National counter-formation in the South.

What is known as the Curragh Mutiny occurred before the outbreak of war and is often cited as the refusal of certain officers to obey orders. It was no such thing. From first to last it was a political development, though largely engineered, as Sir Henry delights to admit, by certain serving officers determined at all costs to baulk the coming legislation. Until the end of 1913 the Unionist party had no wish to solve the particular Ulster problem. They opposed each and every attempt at settlement in their desire, by using Ulster, to wreck the whole measure.

In the review of 1912 Bonar Law himself took the salute with the Ulster leaders when 80,000 Volunteers marched past.

In the spring of 1914 Lord Willoughby de Broke put about the idea that the Lords should refuse to pass the Army Annual Act, thus depriving the Government of any disciplined force. Looking back on the European situation at this date, it appears completely unbelievable that the responsible leader of the opposition could support such an idea. Yet Bonar Law became its leading advocate. This forced even the indecisive Mr. Asquith to take action. Major-General Sir Arthur Paget, C. in C. in Ireland, was instructed to reinforce the troops in Ulster. Before doing this, he received permission from the Minister for War to make certain concessions to the officers who were to carry out these orders. Any officers domiciled in Ulster might, if their units were ordered North, be allowed temporarily to " disappear ". Officers not so domiciled who would not obey would be ordered to resign their commissions. Instead of approaching the commanders privately, Paget summoned a large conference of officers, placing before them a picture of Civil War and coercion.

General Hubert Gough, his brother, John, and some 56 out of 70 cavalry officers said that if this order were given they would " prefer to accept dismissal ".

However unfortunate for the army prestige, the decision was not mutiny, it was a straight answer to a hypothetical situation, which should not have been presented. It was never suggested that troops were being sent to Ulster primarily *to preserve order* and prevent worse trouble. It was implied to them that they were to be instructed to force an unwilling minority. The three leading officers were called to Whitehall, where they were advised covertly on every step to be taken against the Government by its own servant, Sir Henry Wilson. At Whitehall Gough and the others insisted on being given a signed assurance, initialled by the War Minister and Sir John French, that they could not be called on " to enforce the present Home Rule Bill in Ulster ".

Ensor writes : " If it be mutiny to conspire to paralyse from within the disciplined action of an army, unquestionably there was such a conspiracy, although the actual officers at the Curragh were not its authors." These men have been so much criticized, and through them the Army also, that the political engineers behind the scenes have been overlooked.

After the event my father, who was an intimate friend of both Gough brothers and to whom any question of refusing to obey orders was unthinkable, had a long letter from Hubert. He said that the dilemma had been staged in such a way that they were forced to reply as they did.

John Gough fell early in the War and Sir Hubert's fame, with his special vindication years afterwards in Parliament, is well known. Everyone may not realise his subsequent devotion to the cause of better relations between England and the post-treaty Governments. In sympathy he was wholly Southern Irish, but Commonwealth. After he retired he was a member of my husband's Masonic Lodge in London and one day he remarked : " You know, Robertson, it's queer, but you and I are looked on as Sinn Feiners here ! "

Let us hope that Mr. Ensor's important testimony on the Curragh has contributed to his second vindication.

Chapter XI

THE PEN AND THE SWORD.

At this time of ferment it is not surprising that the wealth of the Irish Literary Renaissance should have been discovered and then gone to our heads. It was not new, the novelty was its rediscovery at this moment. It had been latent during the 19th Century and was far more Anglo-Irish than native Irish. Although the Ulster Protestants were four times as numerous as those in the South and the Southern Roman Catholics about twenty times, yet neither of these single-minded majorities produced anything commensurate with our minority record.

To Irish Nationalists the political issue was straightforward and had not the same paradoxical challenge that it had to individual Protestants. Moreover in educational advantages we had taken much the bigger share for ourselves. Even that cultivated Roman Catholic, Gavan Duffy, who ran *The Nation*, did not leave a name to equal Mangan or Davis in verse, or John Mitchell in prose. Mitchell had been one of those transported with other Young Irelanders after 1848, and in " Gaol Journal " he produced a classic ; although bitterly anti-English and partisan in his historical work, this grim Unitarian was kindly in actual relations with the English, and was liked by them personally.

To men in this complex mood of political tension, the revelation of the Irish Celtic heritage had come like new wine. Poets and dramatists turned from the cramped parliamentary arena to seek the wider horizons extended to them by Samuel Ferguson, Standish O'Grady and T.

W. Rolleston ; themselves poets as well as scholars and all of the Protestant world. Even those unable to read the originals could drench themselves in the myths, excite themselves on the speculations of pagan and Christian conflict played by characters of outsize scale and, most important, staged in their own countryside. Their familiar lakes and mountains appeared in an enchanted light, or, as it was usually described, twilight. Instead of being dissentient Anglo-Irish these enthusiasts skipped the English interruption to explore a neo-Celtic world. From this exciting fount of inspiration a stream of poetry emerged : Mangan, one of the earliest to be influenced by the Gaelic, Aubrey de Vere, Lionel Johnson, Edward Martyn (the Roman Catholic), Hyde, AE, and John Eglinton and, star above all this brilliant firmament, Yeats. This list is not given to belittle the Irish contribution, but because one must emphasize how deeply native literature is indebted to the Anglo-Irish element.

In the literature of the Gaelic Renaissance, poetry and myth predominate. Irish history is taken to begin with the Gaels, after some hazy speculations on Gaelic origins in Europe. No interest was shown in those they supplanted, although these included those amazing artists who had formed the renowned gold ornaments, admittedly the finest collection of their kind in Europe. Why is this ? One is tempted to wonder whether these successful Gaelic warriors had not foreseen the complications which generations of local settlers present to their conquerors and, therefore, anticipated trouble by leaving none of them alive to sing a song of martyrdom. Anyhow none were left and we have the gold ornaments.

Soon the essentially dramatic urge of the Celtic Renaissance insisted on a stage setting and the first performance of " Countess Cathleen " (Yeats) was given in 1899 in a hall called by the company the "Celtic Theatre". Actors were still difficult to secure, but with W. G. Fay and his amateur players the National Theatre Company development began in 1902 ; squashed into hired halls and working on a financial basis of sixpences, it still contrived an amazing output, with J. M. Synge added to the playwrights. Local appreciation, however, was confined to Protestants and the movement started with active hostility from patriots or the professedly pious. "Countess Cathleen" was assaulted with howls of abuse and it was not until Fay took the company to London and won enthusiastic support from the English Miss Horniman that the Abbey Theatre could be taken and the National Theatre Co. find a home. After that, artistically, it did not look back and won continental *réclame*. Yet at home priest and patriot continued in active protest until the late twenties, scourging the old and the new "paganism" alike. A responsible Dublin weekly in 1925 described Yeats as "an Englishman wherever he may have been born". In a well-known Irish review a writer denounced "Yeats and his school . . . they are foreigners here . . . they are worse than foreigners . . . they simply have no point of contact at all with Ireland save with the very basest." They were, it was said, distinguished by "their rancorous enmity to the Irish people". Oddly enough, the ultra Loyalists did not appreciate their brethren much more. They were thought long haired and theatrical. Later the second Irish Nobel Literary Prize Winner, Bernard Shaw, was expelled from membership of the Wexford Bee Keepers' Society.

From 1910 on we saw the Abbey Company several times in Cork when the writers included Lady Gregory, James Stephens, Lord Dunsany, and from across the border, Rutherford Mayne. The actors were nearly all

Roman Catholic Irish and they showed considerable pluck in presenting the unpopular roles. The vehemence against Yeats was chiefly due to his supposed pagan attitude, a taint that was also attached to AE, whereas Synge was regarded as careless rather than deliberate.

Although he was a kinsman to my own Synge cousins, I never met J.M. As a man he seems to be remembered less to-day than his fellow-dramatists, possibly because he was not as familiar to Dubliners. His work comprised many angles but there was always what he called " timbre " in his poetry, timbre springing from deep and sometimes harsh roots. His own account of the Aran Islands and the hot August Sunday, when he lay in the shade of the only tree and read a book, gives a glimpse of his attitude to his neighbours and of their friendly acceptance of him. A young priest, who had been rowing round the Islands celebrating Mass fasting, stood still and looked down at him. " Well, Mr. Synge ", he said,

" WELL, MR. SYNGE, IF YOU TURN OUT TO BE RIGHT IN THE END, YOU'LL HAVE THE GREAT LAUGH OVER ME."

taking off his hat and mopping his brow, " if you turn out to be right in the end, you'll have the great laugh over me."

As regular Church of Ireland, Hyde and Robinson were accepted as less exotic. It was not, however, until Synge produced " The Playboy of the Western World " that words were changed for brick-bats. The work, which was not conspicuously Gaelic, was rough peasant and proved to be an insult to the country. For nights turmoil raged, but the play went on. At the time I had come up to Dublin with my mother to make our ceremonial curtseys to the Aberdeens. Driving from Kingsbridge, we craned out of the four-wheeler to see the exciting posters. One ran : " Quiet night at the Abbey Theatre. Only three arrests made."

It was about ten years later, in London, that I came to know W. G. Fay, who played Christy Mahon, the Playboy. He had produced a short comedy of mine for the Play Actors at the Court Theatre, and he remained an intimate friend until his death. He told us of their experience that week and of how he felt on the first night when he delivered his provocative line : " I would sooner have her than a row of chosen females standing in their shifts from here to the Eastern World ".

He could hear the audience shuffle in their seats and, at the operative word " shifts ", the hisses began. But gradually the Playboy became too familiar to bother about and it was safe to patch the rents in the torn curtain. Laudatory echoes from abroad overcame home booings and, in time, it became a popular event wherever it was taken in Ireland. Fay, unfortunately, could not work in with Yeats, or more particularly with Lady Gregory and he, with his brother Frank, was the first loss sustained by the company. Yeats always spoke to me most appreciatively of his genius. At one time he combined leading player with the role of stage electrician, and Yeats told me how awkward it was when Fay ignored his cue at rehearsal and was found sitting in a corner balancing a hammer on his chin.

From 1912 until after 1922 the bill, which was frequently to be seen in London, was built up mainly on the original repertoire, spiced by Lady Gregory's comedies and reinforced by some fine naturalistic peasant and farm dramas, notably by Lennox Robinson and T. C. Murray. It is satisfactory that, later on, our first Irish Government did not heed the so-called " patriotic " abuse of the Abbey movement ; the Theatre was duly taken over as National and accorded a subsidy. Even so it is disastrous that the rift with Sean O'Casey — the Protestant — has deprived us of his later masterpieces.

In 1912 I fulfilled the prediction I had made to my mother and became engaged to a civilian. Manning was just on the verge of being qualified as an architect. He was the son of a Scotsman who had married an Irish woman with a place in Co. Carlow. Herbert Robertson had been Conservative member for South Hackney, the only one of that colour in that constituency. He had been defeated in a bizarre contest by Horatio Bottomley in the *débacle* of 1906, after being largely responsible for the framing of George Wyndham's Land Act. Our Crown background was much the same and Manning shared my uneasiness about the intransigent attitude of so many Unionists and our growing concern over the existence of Carson's army.

However, after our marriage in 1912 we forget home and world alarums and gave ourselves a three months tour through Italy and North Africa, staying in Tunisia with my husband's cousin Terence Bourke at Bizerta.

Terence, intimate of Wilfred Blount, was *persona grata*
with the Arabs and took us to see an Aisoweir where the
chief performer trod on and ate broken glass and
swallowed a sword. The latter act one felt could be
achieved by a good conjuror but eating a wine glass was
much more impressive. Massed drum beats worked up

THE CHIEF PERFORMER TROD ON AND ATE BROKEN GLASS AND
SWALLOWED A SWORD.

the audience to appropriate frenzy and others besides the
leading performer also took part. These ceremonies are
partly religious and strangers in Tunisia are rarely invited, although in Algeria they are popular entertainments
for tourists. The contrast between native Tunisia and
French Algeria could plainly be seen in the Arabs where
the latter lacked dignity and were in every way less responsible and independent than the former with their own
Bey. After Christmas in Bizerta, where I was shown the

art of applying red sealing wax to simulate holly berries, we drifted home via Oran and Barcelona. This apparently opulent trip on first class tickets was achieved per Messrs Cook at so low a cost that no one now would believe it !

We started our married life in London in a world as unlike garrison Cork as anything could well be, though political divisions were probably quite as acute.

One of my father-in-law's close friends was old Swift MacNeill, the Nationalist member and a distant relative of Mrs. Robertson. In the British House of Commons political divisions did not affect friendships as they would have done in Ireland and I often went to the Terrace and met people I had only read of before.

It was in this way that we got to know Joseph Devlin. I constantly had tea with him at the House and later, when he worked so hard to get troops for the Ulster Brigade in my father's division, I realised ever more fully his sincerity and drive. He was more Labour than fire-brand patriot and, by his work for the underdog in the Falls division of Belfast, " Wee Joe " was far more deeply dug in personally than were any of the other leading men in Redmond's Party. He described to me his embarrass-ment over the prominent suffrage ladies who had no doubt that he would love to have them up to speak to his large contingent of women workers in the far from salubrious flax side of the linen factories. These rough girls worked half naked in the vats and the earnest visiting lady speakers were agog to address them. They besought Devlin to fix a date. His trouble was that he knew how old fashioned his girls were ; not only would the spectacle of a woman making a public speech shock them pro-foundly, but it would also shake their confidence in him for sponsoring such unsexed freaks. This dilemma had not been fully resolved before the war came to shatter the propriety of even Irish factory girls. Once I pointed out to him another strange anomaly which centuries of discord had not broken. " Look ", I said, " how beautifully the old gentry class get on with the peasants ! " He did not answer. " It's true ", I persisted, " the ordinary Irish country person much prefers me to you ! " Devlin still hesitated, then : " Yes, it's monstrous that they should, but they do."

The existence of a very large Irish parliamentary party — much out of proportion to our population — was the biggest anomaly of all and was due to a kind of conscience complex which was relieved by the British after they had delayed the passing of Catholic Emancipation. Devlin with his Left slant was less out of touch with Liberal policy than was most of Redmond's party ; but he often confessed how deeply he would regret leaving Westminster when Ireland had Home Rule in Dublin.

It is strange how very few of the old M.P.s ever became Members of the Dail.

Reliving the first part of fateful 1914 the state of near hysteria in Ulster can hardly now be credited. With the Liberals in power the risk of Home Rule was certainly near, but most people in England were sympathetic in disliking coercion while they equally objected to the open threats of direct action on the part of the armed Volunteers. English Unionists headed by Galloper Smith thundered to support Carson, while Southern Loyalists nailed their colours to the Ulster mast, believing that there alone did their salvation lie, an illusion which the future was to shatter.

None of this was wasted on an attentive Germany. There was general relief when responsible opinion in England, headed by the King, called for a conference to consider the possibilities of a solution.

The failure of the final constitutional movement in Ireland was a wholly political affair, and there has not even yet been opportunity to assess its place.

Nothing goes out of fashion so absolutely as yesterday's politics and these must include the two Home Rule Bills introduced by Gladstone and sponsored by Parnell. But for his dramatic love story, few English people to-day would remember Parnell, the Protestant Anglo-Irish landowner, who led the Irish party at the crack of the whip. Yet to the brilliant young barrister, T. M. Kettle, he was no icy enigma when he described him :

> " A flaming coal
> Lit at the stars and sent
> To turn the sin of patience from her Soul,
> The Scandal of Content."

Parnell was a constitutionalist but, unlike the Roman Catholic Redmond who succeeded him, he had an intense aversion to England.

To sketch the recent story, both Home Rule Bills, introduced by Gladstone, failed. The first was thrown out in the Commons and the second was rejected by the Lords. The British electorate refused to favour the second at a subsequent General Election. After many years taken up in settling land purchase and other measures, Redmond in 1910 found himself at the centre of the political see-saw, but because of the veto power of the Lords, he could not make a deal with the Tories. Asquith as Liberal Prime Minister, was, by the Irish vote, pledged to re-introduce Home Rule.

But Redmond no longer commanded the block following that had been loyal to Parnell, or indeed to himself, a dozen years before. In politics only the very strong can afford to be generous. Redmond, who as statesman and man was ready to make any concession to Ulster and other Protestants that would get the Bill implemented without bloodshed, was not allowed to be the Irish Botha, which many broadminded men felt was his role.

The Bill introduced by the Liberals in 1912 was a very mild type of the then fashionable Federal solution, and its practical form has stood the test in working, with slight modification, in the Six Counties since 1920 ; but even there they find the power given them is too limited. To the Anglo-Irishman of to-day it would seem too good to be true, but in 1912 lions walked the paths ahead.

The difficulty in assessing so much of our past history is not that it is impossible to understand the other side but that both sides are so intelligible. The passion of the Irishman to manage his own affairs hardly needs restating, but to the average Unionist of that time it seemed that traitors in the original motherland were handing over his person and fortunes to an inefficient, dishonest majority who detested him and his loyalties. He could hardly be blamed for taking this view since the Nationalist press in Dublin, and still more in the Provinces, excelled in vituperative outpourings against his order ; local administration was riddled with favouritism and venalities ; priests too appeared to have immense political power and, worst of all, terrorism lurked in the active ranks of the Irish Republican Brotherhood. The argument that it might be judicious to treat with a moderate man, such as Redmond, seemed to most Unionists, but by no means all, like approaching Beelzebub with an egg-spoon. The few who realised, what now appears obvious, that it was sensible to temporise with the inevitable, were assured that it was not inevitable if only we kept a " united front " alongside Ulster.

To Ulster the idea of handing over their strong, prosperous, solid, Protestant *bloc* to Papists was catastrophic.

Those who maintain that if the Commonwealth connection were to be renewed to-day Ulster would co-operate, overlook the fact that the Ulster Covenant and Volunteers were formed to resist a measure that unequivocally accepted Crown and Empire. Their case was frankly based on the infamy of transferring a substantial Protestant element to Romanist control. That objection was, and still is, their fundamental argument, although " disloyalty " is added as a useful and genuinely effective extra.

The use of the words " religious intolerance " applied to Northern Protestants is probably unfair. Bigotry, there was, but intolerance suggests a desire to dominate another race or creed, the right in fact " to wallop your nigger ". Ulster did not want to wallop, but she did not intend to be the nigger. She may have been mistaken in fearing Roman Catholic supremacy but that was her deeply held conviction and no one is ever going to take in the essence of the *impasse* who does not face up to this reality ; one as significant to-day as it was in 1912-14.

Ulster loyalty to the Crown is a comparatively recent affair. It did not develop until after Catholic Emancipation in 1829, which also gave their Charter of Liberty to Presbyterians. Before it, even their Church marriages were not considered legal. Ulster lands were not theirs by grace of the Crown. James I had grabbed the territories of the Earls who had flown from their own intriguing neighbours, but he was busier prosecuting Dissenters than in pursuing Roman Catholics. Hunted Scotsmen fled from the persecution to Ireland and bought small holdings from the Undertakers there who had purchased the confiscated estates. With Scottish prudence they insisted on a fairer return for their bawbees than the Crown had given to the Southern Irish. This fixity of tenure enabled them to farm well and survive the post-Famine difficulties. They remained rabidly republican, led the '98 Rebellion, and also, which is not so well known, took a leading anti-British part in the Boston Tea Party. The revival of Roman power, which blossomed with Emancipation, produced a dramatic change in the old Covenanters. Anything — even the Crown — was now found to be better than the Papists ; thus the new, strange marriage of convenience was formulated and hallowed.

If Redmond at that date had remained the ' uncrowned King of Ireland " that he had been, some compromise as a temporary expedient might have been tried. Redmond's party, however, was suffering from middle-class middle-age. Its supporters were largely composed of the well-to-do established shopkeepers and farmers, out of touch with the group of young educated men which had succeeded Smith O'Brien's Young Ireland movement and, backed by Gaelic fervour and Labour influences, hankered for complete separation. Most important of all, the country was comparatively prosperous. There is much truth in O'Connell's words that Ireland never rebels on an empty stomach.

Redmond was not only acquiescent to staying inside the British Empire, he preferred it. He and his brother William were both married to loyal Australians and his ardent ambition was to emphasise the extent to which Ireland had shared in building that Empire. He felt the injustice that more credit had not been given to her contribution ! It is now clear that he underrated the influence of the young separatist element. Nevertheless he had taken the less extreme of the Volunteers under the aegis of the Parliamentary party and they were now recognised as National, with himself as official leader.

They too were prepared to accept him while he seemed useful. But his new, very shaky, adherents would never have tolerated any settlement that *excluded a part of Ulster*. That idea was comparatively novel and had only been worked up after the discussion on the first Home Rule Bill. There had always been faction feuds with Ulster but they had not before been a problem. It did not occur to the Nationalists then — and it does not now — that it was their own extreme attitude which had helped to make the problem. The myths dividing the two peoples are not just the same thing seen in reverse. The Southern Irishman claims that the whole island is sacred, indivisible soil ; the Northerner sees the affair as human, as his particular freedom ; he is less interested in geography.

So many people of good-will in England disapproved of both private armies that in May 1914 — probably as a consequence of a recent successful gun-running into Ulster — the Conservatives thought it politic to show compromise. They brought in an amendment permitting the predominantly Protestant areas (not as large as the present Six Counties) to coopt out. If this were to be accepted they promised to support and encourage the Irish Parliament.

But Asquith's vacillation had so much weakened Redmond that he could not now accept this genuine chance of peace. Asquith had refused to recognise that Ulster had a case, yet he allowed her to form and arm a large army. Then, alarmed by the coming threat of two armies, he decreed that no arms at all were to be allowed into Ireland, thus most unjustly leaving Ulster with a monopoly.

The conference called by the King in July, while clouds blackened the world, effected no understanding or cure.

Before the month was out the National Volunteers

brought off a highly successful landing of arms. Police and military interference led to firing, and civilians fell with belligerents on the Quay at Bachelor's Walk in Dublin.

Temperatures were soaring, but on August 4th the world situation was transformed by the outbreak of War.

To the great relief of all those who dreaded internal rebellion Redmond made his momentous speech in the House of Commons, pledging Ireland to the cause of Western Europe and co-operation in the war. His courage was remarkable as the speech was made on the day of the inquests on the Martyrs of Bachelor's Walk.

The man whom Englishmen had regarded as a predatory eagle now offered them the olive branch in his beak.

In return for this gesture the Home Rule Bill, without amendment, became an Act, but was not to become operative until the war was over. Neither side was satisfied, but reasonable people everywhere welcomed the breathing space which general calamity had brought to Ireland. For Redmond everything now depended on confirming a most hazardous position, which could only be justified by success ; if he failed he would be branded as a traitor to his country. Ulster, equally apprehensive, was resolved to show England that Redmond's new-found support was deliberate bluff to discount honest Ulster's enthusiasm to serve England. This belief was held whole heartedly and accounts for much of the subsequent behaviour.

Redmond, desperate to attract Irish support, proposed that Ireland should form a new version of its traditional Irish Brigade, famous in Europe since Sarsfield. When Kitchener's army was propounded the XVIth Disision was allotted to Ireland and Redmond promised that he would fill its ranks. My father, now a retired Lt. General, was appointed by Lord Kitchener to raise it from its Head-quarters in Mallow, Co. Cork. He was then a very active man of 64, well known for his aptitude for training and for gaining the sympathy of his subordinates. My mother, very fortunately, went over to join him in Mallow.

My husband had been rejected for service owing to the rheumatic fever he had while at Magdalen and I was spared the ordeal of his going overseas. The first War, to anyone brought up in the Garrison world, was annihilation. Wave after wave of our relations and friends disappeared. I sometimes wonder whether those young men I had known in India and Cork, and who followed the single and uncomplicated ideals they believed in, did not for all their ordeals fare better than their sons in the second War who, with equal gallantry, died for what few of them could define. Many of them were uncertain of their own doubts. Youth is not supposed to know but, unless it thinks it does, its plight is pitiable.

Chapter XII

THE LAST IRISH DIVISION.

On his way to Ireland in November 1914, my father had a talk with Lord Kitchener. Both agreed that they understood Irishmen ; an initial mistake, for no one who does so would be bold enough to think it.

At that time muddle and chaos were rife in all the newlyborn head-quarters. The first ten divisions were naturally given the best men then available and the 10th division was also named as an Irish division, although not specifically the one with which Redmond's Irish Brigade was to be identified. Most available Irish officers joined it, however, as it was formed before the XVIth.

In the all round scramble it was extremely difficult to get suitable Colonels and Company Commanders and the contradictory problem of securing men who were both suitable as soldiers and attractive politically raised thorns. My father was quite without religious prejudice, which unfortunately implied that he was not primarily interested in obtaining Roman Catholics. Frankly, he minded very little what religion they professed. He had been deeply disgusted over the Curragh incident and resolved that no " damned politicians " should interfere with, or jeopardise, the lives of his soldiers by insisting on inappropriate, inefficient appointments. With good men at a discount he was inclined to prefer an experienced senior officer who was not an Irishman to someone with a useful political background, but who seemed to him likely to be incompetent in the field or in training other men. Recruiting for the ranks was at first fairly satisfactory and the general feeling in favour of the War was far greater in the country generally than Sinn Feiners will now allow. All arrangements for R.C. Chaplains and their services were carried out in complete accord with Dr. Browne, then Roman Catholic Bishop of Cloyne, from whom my father received numerous appreciative letters. Throughout his connection with the Division the respect and affection shown to him by officers and men was outstanding.

The Ulster politicians could all command influence and their *protegés* profited. Why, complained the Nationalists, were they not favoured in the same way? It is perhaps easy for those accustomed to the old Army to understand that practically all Ulstermen of officer standing had had some form of military training, even at school in the O.T.C. The Nationalist type had not. Very few of them were public-school men, or looked like such, and in 1914 public schools were recognised as arsenals for young officers. To us now, after learning how limited generals drawn solely from one class could be, this prejudice appears archaic, but it must be remembered that the pre-war Army was one based on training for the Field. Total war strategy did not exist. The average pre-war " Tommy " was not well educated and he probably did prefer the then officer class more than his critical contemporary would to-day. On the Continent it was not questioned that the British junior officer was an enviable asset. What was thought of seniors and staff was less rosy.

To resolve the commission difficulty, as he fully believed, my father started a well staffed Cadet Training Company in the Connaught Rangers. All aspirants for commissions enlisted and were placed in the Cadet Company, to be translated when found worthy. It was fair and democratic and, as a means of training officers, it could not have been more satisfactory nor, for the majority, more popular. But as a political device for a distracted leader trying to entice M.P.s, J.P.s, touchy publicans, and financial supporters to send their sons to an extremely dangerous and not very popular war it was, to say the least of it, rebuffing. Elsewhere Redmond knew that loyal allies in and out of the Empire were boosting their propaganda by every type of inducement, privilege and push. In the XVI Division, as commanded by my father, push or pull did not exist. Redmond's own son was told by his general, who had found him a bit haughty, that he must set an example to the others and enlist in the Cadet Company ; whereat he used both push and pull elsewhere and received a commission in the Irish Guards. He served in this critical regiment with great distinction, but his loss as an inducement to other young men of his type to join the XVI Division was considerable.

Redmond's own brother, that gallant gentleman William, was as a senior man at once awarded the rank of Company Commander, but I know my father was terrified, for his sake and the men under him, lest his eminently unwarlike habit of mind should, when tried in the field, land them all into casualties. Actually he did extremely well in the somewhat static trench warfare.

Throughout these difficult days nothing could exceed the unselfish tact of that delightful *littérateur*, Stephen Gwynn, who stayed with my parents the night before he shaved off his civilian beard. He was that rarity, a Protestant Nationalist M.P., and, as a man of European habit, was single-hearted against the enemy. He was devoted to his political chief and also became personally attracted and attached to my father. He fully realised

the opposing ideals of the politician and the soldier and
has recorded the conflict, most fairly, in his book " The
Last Years of John Redmond ". I think it surprised him
that any general could personally be as humble and simple
as my father. He warmly extended the same affection
to my mother, whose sympathy with Redmond's task was
unbounded. It was only lately that she had become
interested in theoretical politics, for which, however, she
had a unusual flair. She complained that she had spent
three-quarters of her life obsessed by hats and hunting.
Later it was hats — *always most becoming ones* — and
politics. From the first she realised that the success of
the Division at home, and with it Redmond's prestige here,
was infinitely more important to Ireland than its military
efficiency, a point of view which scandalised my father.

The crux occurred when Redmond requested the War
Office to recognise the National Volunteers. I am glad
to say that my father believed you had either to " trust
the fellows " — which I admit he did not do with complete enthusiasm — or disband them. It was clear that
Lord Kitchener's knowledge of Irishmen, on which he
still prided himself, made him too mistrustful to concede.
My father, who had been summoned to London to
discuss the matter, insisted that recognition would involve
some semblance of control and was far the least dangerous
course — Kitchener, being constitutionally undecided,
put off making a decision, and fatally there was no
recognition.

My mother urged my father to tell Redmond how
strongly he, personally, believed in recognition and
realised that the position of this hostile body of men
adversely affected recruiting and the general Irish outlook
on the War. I know that my father did agree but not
strongly enough to speak out personally and back a

political policy not approved at the War office. If he, as the man on the spot coming from the loyalist class, could have brought himself openly to encourage recognition. it must have strengthened Redmond enormously. By his lack of ardour and defiance he gave Redmond the impression that he did not trust the Volunteers, or more hurtful because partly true, Redmond's influence over them ; but my father really did believe that to leave this body armed and unrecognised, was leading inevitably to bloodshed.

To this day no one can say with any conviction quite where recognition would have led, but it might have averted the 1916 outbreak and even the later Troubles and disastrous Civil War. To leave these enthusiastic young men unused extinguished any influence Redmond might have retained. If Asquith had had the strength of mind to free Kitchener from the onus of making the decision, and had himself insisted on recognition, Kitchener would probably have been glad to escape from the personal responsibility.

My father considered that for him personally to back Redmond in some prominent manner would be melodramatic and unsoldierly.

Alongside these troubles there was the pressure of Ulster's friends ; no one connected with the control of the XVI Division had any doubt that certain forces at the War Office were working against it. Sir Henry Wilson was in France, but it is understandable that others with his views were well placed and that they were hardly likely to have wasted their chances when Kitchener was under petition from Redmond. It did not occur to them that they were acting disloyally in time of war. What use was that " Irish Brigade " anyhow ? Why waste good materials when others needed them more ? With the Home Rule Act on the statute book Redmond must not get away with his so-called " loyal " bluff ; he must not be allowed to appear sincere when obviously he was not.

There were numerous pin pricks and all of them reacted on recruiting. The division got its rifles and uniforms later than anyone else and the Sinn Feiners jeered at those training in ugly overalls with wooden rifles, months after they had enrolled. The Volunteers had neat uniform and no reticence in parading their lethal arms. These may have been departmental accidents ; such cannot be claimed for the fact that my father passed through the Ulster divisional lines, to inspect his Northern Catholic Brigade, without being saluted by a single Ulster officer although he was wearing his full rig-out. This was his lesson for being a renegade, commanding Papists.

Later the divisional musketry butts in England had to be whitewashed, causing a day's delay before the XVI Division were allowed to enter them. The effect of so many slogans, " To hell with the Pope and the XVI Division," left purposefully by the Ulstermen, was not considered edifying by the English officers in charge.

I do not repeat this tittle-tattle to recall unpleasantness — the two divisions got on excellently in France — but to show the extravagance to which suspicion and apprehension can reduce reasonable people. That was over forty years ago. How different are their sons to-day? And how much do the sons of those once in the XVI division realise the character of the people they profess to woo, but yet exasperate ?

Meanwhile the formation and training of the Division went on, always harassed by the necessity for wasting the time of serving officers on recruiting efforts. When I was staying with my parents I took advantage of my strategic position to find out if I could secure some special Irish posters. The Chief Recruiting Officer gave me a copy of every poster then in use in Ireland. Except for one, all were of the prevailing British type. I have them now, " If the Cap Fits ", " What did you do in the Great War, Father ? ", Kitchener pointing his finger, and the whole lot familiar to those days. The one local exception was small and insignificant, laughably inadequate in its appeal and its naive attempt to weave Shamrock with Union Jack, and English King with Irish Country.

Every returned officer likely to be a draw was pounced on to make stirring appeals at meetings, where " God save the King ", the Unionist theme song, was invariably played. One of these young men risen to be captain and winner of the V.C. had been a ranker. He was sent to address his home town at Bantry, where he had once served at Bantry House as the Leigh-Whites' footman. They were delighted to entertain him but felt faintly uncertain as to how their rather pompous butler, Barnett, would like having to wait on him at dinner. He, however, told the young man that he owed all his advancement to the " proper " training he had received in the pantry. The V. C. agreed and the party went with a bang.

Curiously enough there was always a good intake of Northern Roman Catholics collected by Joe Devlin, the only member of the old Parliamentary party who kept his footing when the slide began ; this, I am sure, was largely because of his influence with labour. Let it not be forgotten that the Sinn Fein Volunteers and early supporters were first recruited from Liberty Hall and led by Pearse and Larkin.

Both the Redmonds and Gwynn worked unceasingly to raise the required quota and Professor T. M. Kettle was one of the most successful. He was a young man of rare intellect who treated aid to France against the barbarian as a personal crusade. He was not a man for whom army life was easy and my father who was interested in the civilians' adjustments was able to befriend him in many small ways.

In the autumn of 1915 the Division was moved for its final three months of burnishing to a camp outside Aldershot. I have seen letters from the Under-Secretary of War, many General Inspecting Officers and Divisional Orders testifying to the high morale and discipline attained.

Redmond, John Dillon and T. P. O'Connor used to come down to us very often but, although they respected my father, he and they were a bit shy of each other. It was definitely my mother's open devotion to Ireland and her ever present wit which made things congenial ; that and my parents' naturally devotional attitude when Cardinal Bourne came to give a special blessing to the divisional arms.

Now aged 65 and as a Lieut.-General, my father was not eligible for a divisional command in the field. Major-General W. B. Hickie, a Roman Catholic, was appointed to take the division overseas. In view of my father's efforts he was, however, asked to remain and lead the march past at the King's Farewell Inspection. No one could have been more sympathetic than the new Commander, who even selected my father's initials as a monogram for the divisional badge.

The King's riding accident prevented him from being present so Queen Mary deputized, bringing with her the young Duke of York and Princess Mary. My father's first question to the Queen was, of course, to enquire for the King and he added that he regarded the danger of a

horse rearing back as one of the most unpleasant
accidents that could happen. Queen Mary became
surprisingly excited. " I *am* glad you say that. Do you
know they're all making out he fell off ! ". Fortunately
my father had had a first hand account of the mishap,
but one wonders at the temerity of those who had passed
on the affront to Queen Mary of all people ! Her interest
in every Irish personality impressed my father who stood
beside her on the saluting base and told her who was who.

They made a marvellously good show this last grand
parade of Irish crowned troops, headed by pipers and
their decorative wolf hounds. Battalions of all the
historic Irish regiments were there, unconscious of how
soon they were destined for Limbo. After the treaty all
but the two Ulster regiments were extinguished.

Such a change was inevitable but left sad memories.
Anyone who has experienced the personal good feeling,
camaraderie and common humanity of regimental life in
peace and war must regret the extinction of a fighting unit.
There was no place where the Crown and Harp formed
a single symbol so sincerely as on a Regimental badge or
button. The unity was voluntary, not imposed, and the
men of various origins in the Dublins or the Rangers spilt
their blood on many battlefields and won renown for
Irishmen.

The stormy events, which began in 1916 and continued
through the unsuccessful convention of 1917, ended all
that, just as truly as the failure of his hope caused the
death of John Redmond in January 1918.

William Redmond, after a deeply dramatic return and
speech to the House of Commons, was killed amongst his
men in 1917, uncertain if his particular work for his
country would prevail. Perhaps it did not fail as conspicuously as his countrymen try to assert. Many people

believe that without it England would have been more reluctant to accept the Truce in 1921. If it takes two to make a war, it also takes two to make a peace.

To us, and most especially to my mother, William's death was a personal sorrow. He wrote to her very often from the trenches and promised to send a German souvenir captured by the Division. There came an 18-pounder brass shell case with a silver mount bearing the inscription : " Picked up at Guillemont and given to Lady Parsons by Major William Redmond as a token that the XVI Irish Division does not forget L. P.   September 1916." The initials were described in the monogram form that was used as the divisional badge.

Tom Kettle fell at Ginchy on September 9th 1916 aged 36. The events of Easter Week in Ireland only confirmed his conviction that Ireland had to side with Europe. His pacifist brother-in-law, Francis Sheehy-Skeffington, had been murdered by an insane British officer during the affray in Dublin and Kettle was racked by the trend of thought and action during the weary days before his death.

The bust of this brave man is now in St. Stephen's Green.* For some years Nationalist prejudice prevented it from being so honoured and its pedestal stood empty.

On September 4th on the battlefield he wrote a sonnet addressed to his little daughter, which lifts the ordeal into the only realms where such events can be endured :

To my daughter Betty, the Gift of God.

In wiser days, my darling rosebud, blown
To beauty proud, as was your mother's prime.
In that desired, delayed, incredible time,
You'll ask me why I abandoned you, my own,
And the dear heart that was your baby throne,
To dice with death. And oh ! they'll give you rhyme

And reason ; some will call the thing sublime,
And some decry it in a knowing tone.
So here, while the mad guns curse overhead,
And tired men sigh, with mud for couch and floor,
Know that we fools, now with the foolish dead,
Died not for flag, nor King, nor Emperor,
But for a dream, born in a herdsman's shed,
And for the secret Scripture of the poor.

*Since this chapter was written, the bronze bust, forty
years after Kettle's death, was thrown into the lake in the
Green, but it has survived the indignity and been reinstated
once more.

CHAPTER XIII

SWORD UNSHEATHED.

Although the Dublin Rising of 1916 is taken as the epitome of the action against Britain, it was only a single event, lasting for less than a week and ending in capitulation. The cause of its immense influence lay first in the glamour of the shock tactics whereby the British Army, even if only a skeleton force, was openly defied, and, secondly, in the martyrdom of those executed. Had the British retribution, natural to any country which felt itself stabbed in the back during a bitterly critical war, been more severe, but quick and summary, it would not have aroused the same savage resentment. As it was, the careful legal impartiality, so dear to the British, used in defining each of the long drawn out convictions, turned every young man and woman into a successor of the deceased. The accused were not treated as the soldiers they felt themselves to be, but as common criminals. The British plea that they were rebelling against their own people and their own brothers in the field was nullified by the abrogation of Irish civil law. Admittedly Irish Courts at that time could not have handled the offences any better than they did later under two Irish governments, but their failure would have thrown the onus on to the right shoulders, creating a responsible public opinion, instead of one almost unanimously anti-British and anti-Redmond.

If the Irish Courts had not convicted the sixteen accused men, the British sense of injury would have been less serious than the subsequent loss of prestige suffered. The failure of the Convention and Redmond's fall and death early in 1918 was followed almost at once by the abortive policy of trying to apply conscription to Ireland. It was the final attempt to impose what was genuinely considered " fair " on to a basically unfair national situation.

By the end of the European war the links of loyalty binding many Irishmen to soldiers serving overseas no longer held ; moreover large numbers of these soldiers on returning home joined the insurgents. Middle-class public opinion, which before April 1916 had been against physical disturbance, was now sympathetic, often active.

Thus the end of the War, which everywhere else was a tremendous relief, brought increased tension to Ireland, still faced by statutory Home Rule that was due to become operative. Sir Henry Wilson and Ulster prepared for battle. No one blames Ulster for taking every reasonable precaution against a measure which every man jack abominated actually to the death. In this desire for protection England was behind them. Where it was not behind them was in the threat of armed resistance. It was realised that such a threat was bound to react on Southern Ireland, as indeed it did.

I only once saw Sir Henry at close quarters. When my father took me to the Artillery Memorial Service at St. Paul's he sat in the row in front of us. His was an extraordinary face, as though Caran D'ache had hacked it out of old rough deal. When I read the famous diary, it came vividly back to mind. His outpourings showed such triviality and rancour. His detestation of Southern Ireland was far stronger than any loyalty to Ulster and this was, of course, only too well known and returned. The tale on both sides made up an anthology of hate, culminating in that grim scene when, as he returned to his London home, two young men shot him on his own door-step. Typical to the last, he lived long enough to draw his sword and died with it in his hand. The men, who ran off shooting, were followed by the inhabitants of the whole street and were caught. They proved to be unimportant members of the I.R.A. who had drawn this special Killing lot. The Jurors in the trial were threatened dramatically and everything was done to terrorise, but to no avail. The effect in England and Ulster exceeded anything the murdered man could have wished for.

About five years ago I happened to be present at a local farming conference held during holiday time in an R. C. Theological College. As we waited for the lecturer, I glanced round the white distempered walls of the class room. A few very bad oil pictures hung round it. The one nearest me depicted Henry Wilson, drawn sword and all, about to fall. His wife was shown looking out by the curtain from the window.

The anthology of hate was evidently still alive, although I cannot believe that it was widely shared by the young men plying their biros at their Christian studies.

It is, however, a distressing fact that anti-British feeling should be the active factor that it still is. It is hate of the British, not dislike to the Northerner, that has made young men in the 1950's volunteer to cross and fire over the Border. The English act that partitioned us is blamed, not the real cause of Protestant resistance. What is it that feeds this hate now that the British have left?

By 1919 the resistance campaign was replanned, not on the basis of *coup d'état* but of undermining all channels of authority. Every weapon of terror, intimidation, and appropriation was accepted. The first objective was to clear out the police from the smaller barracks and, by burning and assaults, to force them into larger and more central concentrations. Soon no official eyes or ears were left in the country districts. Mails, transport, banks, were continually held up and robbed ; small military detachments were ambushed. Unionists' houses were burnt, but not often pillaged ; above all, anybody in authority, civil or military, connected with information or intelligence was assassinated. The British never modified their attitude that no " war " existed, nor the Irish their right to kill whom and where they could. The introduction of reprisals, which meant burning the houses of humble civilians whom the British thought should have reported " incidents ", added to the unreality. The same cottages were practically always the property of Unionists whose own houses were, more often than not, burnt in counter reprisal. The Military were not under Castle rule, and War Office reluctance to employ the Regular Army for actual suppression still held. Troops were quartered to preserve order but took little direct action in engagements.

On the whole the Irregulars did not grossly antagonise the soldiers and in many districts British forces, bored by the situation, allowed rifles and ammunition to be commandeered and stolen, thus repeating what Spencer described as :

> " Where they see laws more slackely tended . . . they grow more loose and careless of their duty."

It is flattering themselves for the British to regard their well known acceptance of order as a superior quality inherent in their blood. For nearly a thousand years the fortune of history has spared them from invasion at home and they have gradually been enabled to build up a protective edifice of law to which they have become accustomed. Yet even this habit is not proof against exceptional provocation, especially if it occurs in Ireland! It was not only the soldiers who bartered their arms ; in 1920 the British Government, exasperated by the Irish

method of warfare, decided to copy it, only more drastically. A tough Auxiliary Police Force was formed for the
express purpose and sent to Ireland " to treat the Rebels
with their own medicine." It has been pleaded that the
idea was not English but the invention of a vindictive
Welshman, Lloyd George. Actually the " Black-and-
Tans " (named from the black berets they wore with their
khaki uniforms) were nearly all English and were
commanded by an Englishman. The record that they
left in Cork is enough to condemn both the policy and its
interpretation. On one single night in St. Patrick Street,
about fifty large shops were burnt out. In the subsequent
debate in the Commons no single English member believed that such a deed could be the work of any but
Irishmen. The government, with hand on breast,
promised an immediate enquiry and to publish the full
Report. The enquiry was held at once under the
Presidency of the Officer Commanding in Cork, Major-
General Strickland. After the evidence had been ex-
amined, the Report was duly forwarded. From that day
no detail of the finding has been revealed. It was in the
" public interest " to hold it back ! Everyone living in
Cork either saw or knew who the delinquents were ; none
of these were recalled. The English public was spared
the ordeal of hearing the truth and the Government of
risking the exposure of its gullibility in swallowing the
childish clues that were first laid. The incident was soon
forgotten in England but, in Ireland, even the generous
compensation paid out of English taxes has not erased the
memory.

Because the British refused to recognise the fighting
against them as legal war, all their fatal losses were
ranked as cases of " murder ", meriting death by hanging.
Less heinous offences were treated in internment camps

and these became clubs for more effective insurrection. Adequate protection was not given to officials who were obvious targets for attack, and Unionists who were unpopular were ranked by the Irish as Britain's allies.

Repellent incidents on both sides are only too easy to recall, such as the shooting of old Mrs. Lindsay and her coachman or the trigger happy outbreaks of the Black and Tans. Such examples of inhumanity do not cancel each other out ; added together they double the horror for those who remember them.

But with rare exceptions in certain badly disaffected districts, especially where irregulars from a distance interfered, landlords, who got on well with their neighbours, generally escaped lightly. Many were suspected of contributing privately to local Sinn Fein funds. For several years no police had functioned and the representatives of the S. F. movement made themselves responsible for local order. We personally were thankful we were never asked to subscribe, as at that time my husband was High Sheriff for Co. Carlow, the last to be appointed. It was not an enviable position as it was supposed to be his privilege to attend hangings. Until the Truce, however, he was too busy in his official post in England to be released for Assizes and we only came over for our holidays.

Except for having to take cover in doorways in Dublin during ambushes, we were fortunate in suffering very little. During the queer stagnant pause betwen Truce and Treaty we had 60 men billeted for about six weeks here in our house, in the yard, and out-houses. Thirty officers, as it happened of the roughest type, lived in the house, then unoccupied by the family. Both the private chapel and the cellar, fuller than it is now, were placed by the O.C. as *out of bounds*. The local Roman Catholic

Curate called every day during the occupation and saw
to it that boots were wiped, carpets lifted, and needless
damage avoided. Only my store of jam was eaten and
the piano had to be refelted after much playing of jazz.
At the end of the occupation all the blankets were washed
by order. One offender, who had stolen apples, passed
a frightened hour as prisoner in the dungeon and it is
related that the " roars of him would terrify you ! "
Later on, during the Civil War, a regular force of Free
Staters billeted for a short time and the Commandant
wrote an account of the local situation in the Visitors'
Book, ending " de Valera still at large '. Years after, my
husband unexpectedly found a detonator amongst his
music in the drawing room and we still keep the pot in
which lead for bullets was melted in the same room.

Perhaps our immunity was somewhat due to the
personality of the exceptional butler and his family ; perhaps still more to the good name which my husband's
forebear, an astute old Alexander Durdin, had built up
during the disturbances of '98. Memories are long and
I wonder how often during the troubled years I was told
of how, when Alexander returned from a visit to Dublin,
he found nine local villagers hanging from the great lime
trees of the avenue, followed by the inevitable comment,
" Mr. Durdin was very much annoyed about it ! " This
was not the entertaining under-statement that it sounds —
annoyance in 18th Century English meant fury.

I do not propose to discuss the individual events or
personalities of those days. At the time much of it was
relieved by incidents of grim comedy as when we heard
of a desperate young man — " bowed down with bombs ";
but the loss of so many lives and homes was too tragic for
laughter.

It is part of the distortion of such events that civilised

people can get together and solemnly analyse the ethics of assassination and dishonesty. Why should it be worse to leave one small bomb in a suitcase in a cloakroom than to drop a larger one at random from the sky? Why is it worse to shoot one policeman from behind a hedge than to ambush a column of soldiers on a road? What is the moral difference between robbing a bank to finance a cause and commandeering a nation's securities? Leaving ethical principle aside, experience shows that the practical distinction rests in the subsequent reaction on one's own side. A demobilised regular army goes home to Civvy street and thankfully forgets the war, while the swords carried by *Francs Tireurs,* resistance forces and irregular armies are double edged, suicidal to those who wield them. Such swords undercut social order and are not easily sheathed.

To give an example of how much consciences harden, I remember, as early as in 1917, arriving in Ireland and asking our dignified station-master how things were. " Quite quiet over here ", was the reply, " only shooting an odd policeman ".

The methods used against the British during the Troubles were directly responsible for the fratricidal Civil War that followed the departure of British troops from Ireland. To the rank and file of the Irish insurgents the enormous difference in the terms given by the British in 1921 from those previously doled out to the constitutional Redmond seemed a clear victory for Force. But circumstances had changed. In 1917 Britain was fighting a precarious campaign and was afraid that if this country were free to do so, it would join the enemy. Therefore only limited concessions could be granted. Four short years later, continental danger was past and Britain was impatient to cut losses and achieve good-will near home.

Unlike their followers, the I.R.A. leaders were well aware
that they had not won the war, but they knew they had
created a nuisance value, causing undue expense to
Britain at home and misunderstanding abroad.

In the grim interval before the Truce, the tension experienced by those of us with our homes over here was
exhausting. We were pledged to uphold order and we
deplored force but the British policy, or lack of it, forced
us to be partisans of Britain and so liable to be pitched
into the abyss. We had no protection and, if the situation
had continued, there would not have been a Unionist
house left. Clearly a settlement would have to be made.

Sir Samuel Hoare, Air Minister, (afterwards Lord
Templewood) was an old friend of my husband ; he was
known to be associated with certain English churchmen
working for peace. Manning decided to write to him
emphasising our miserable predicament in being linked
with the British policy and begging him to use his influence to do something for us. Sir Sam at once replied
that he could not agree more but that he saw no chance
of convincing his colleagues in the Cabinet. The same
week General Sir John Maxwell went over from Dublin,
and proved that what Sir Sam thought impossible
would after all have to be conceded by the Cabinet. This
shows the nature of the hand to mouth British policy.

The price of restoring order, as presented by the British
military authorities in 1921, was so excessive that the
Cabinet decided to make a real effort to secure peace.
The Irish leaders realised that this was their last effective
bargaining chance, and that the " order " to be enforced
in the event of failure would be obliterating. All responsible parties saw that the advantages of peace were
imperative.

The Truce which arose was an overwhelming relief to

the mass of the exhausted country, longing for normality. Unfortunately, the year which followed it, before the Treaty was framed, only gave second wind to the Irregulars, triumphant that they had won victory and shamed the Redmondites. To compromise now by accepting the Treaty terms seemed not only unnecessary, but a betrayal of the sword.

Opposition to the Treaty was also voiced by the back-woodsmen among the Irish Unionists, although their official leaders had advocated its acceptance as the only constructive policy. These people sincerely believed that this surrender to force was immoral, an open encouragement of the murder which the Government had defined the "war" to be. Had these Unionists previously suggested a conciliatory policy of reason their argument might have stood up. As it was, the half case fell down on the contradiction that all the time she had been in Ireland Britain had consistently imposed force. Where the Unionists deplored the type of force used they had a better case, but the crooked sword about to be unsheathed again was to affect them less than it did Nationalists, although some of them, like their most distinguished representative Sir Horace Plunkett, were to lose their homes in the ensuing turmoil.

Except as single targets the tale was not one in which the Anglo-Irish as a body was involved. The noted individual extremists, Madame Maude Gonne, Madame Markievicz (née Gore-Booth), Lord Midleton's sister — Albreda Broderick and Mrs. Despard, sister of Lord French, continued to the last as die-hard Republicans. Most of the others who had joined in the Anti-British fight were pulled by the forces of their traditional impulses to favour restored order and, therefore, accept the Treaty. Erskine Childers, an exception, sided with Mr.

de Valera and was shot after the rift occurred ; he was
an instance of an Anglo-Irishman who served England
against Germany but Ireland against England, a complication by no means unique.

Amongst the recorders of both wars three writers of
Anglo-Irish families have told the tale well.   Frank
Pakenham, now Lord Pakenham in the Labour Party, in
" Peace through Ordeal ", Terence de Vere White in his
life of Kevin O'Higgins and Arland Ussher in a short
but brilliant analysis : " The Face and Mind of Ireland ".
Anyone interested in the period should turn to these
books.

If the old gentry made many and bad mistakes, as
these books confirm, no generation of men in these islands
has paid for them and for their past privileges more
dearly.   All their manhood went ungrudgingly as
volunteers to the two World Wars ; many had their
homes burnt and pillaged, they were shot at and they
had to submit to a *régime* of which they whole-heartedly
disapproved.   They have since lost their rôle in the
voluntary administration of the country to which they
had been accustomed, and have gradually accepted their
lot with a practical common sense derived from a long
secure position and serving of order.

Many of them took advantage of the good compensation
they received for the loss of their homes and left the
country.   Far more remained.   If they had to rebuild,
they generally did so near but not on the same site, perhaps creating some envy in their neighbours who occupied
larger and much more inconvenient houses.   People
attribute this persistence to remain in Ireland to their
love of sport, still obtainable here, or to their dislike of
the more democratic social atmosphere of England and
to the lower income tax.   I think the real answer is that

the centuries had made them happier here than they are elsewhere ; the attraction of familiar people and scenery and the easier tempo of life suits them. Those who left were mostly coerced away by their wives, and when seen at Cheltenham and the like are stated to look rather lost and forlorn.

Arland Ussher makes merry of the old " Colonels ", too purblind to recognise the political context, or the hopelessness of old values. He does not do justice to their most conspicuous effort made at a difficult moment after the Treaty was signed, and with the guns of the civil war echoing in the provinces.

There was found to be no adequate setting available for the new Parliament, the Dail. The Royal Dublin Society, the special child of the leading " Colonels ", was in possession of the beautiful Leinster House in an enviable site in central Dublin. Here they kept their library and gave their concerts, holding their celebrated Horse Show outside the city at Ballsbridge, where their vast show yard buildings were situated. They were asked at almost a moment's notice whether they would agree to give up Leinster House and park themselves in head quarters in Ballsbridge until such time as the Government would provide them with new accommodation there. The Council met. Protests from the back-woods must have deafened them. To move out of the City Boundaries " meant the end of the Society ". After the meeting, the Government was informed that the Royal Dublin Society acceded to the request.

Because the consequences worked out so favourably, let the decision not be forgotten nor the moment at which it was made. The Dail had the advantage of starting its life in dignified historic surroundings. The R.D.S. became a first charge on the new *régime*. Fresh blood was

added to the Council, but the "Colonels" were not
swamped ;   the   various   Departments   of   Defence,
Agriculture, Commerce and Education concerned themselves with its success.

When we arrived in Dublin in 1925 the fine new
buildings were already practically completed.   The
library was larger, to meet the much larger membership,
the concerts even better, and much better attended and,
since such practical matters count for much, the Society's
funds grew so healthily that it can now afford to send its
lecturers all over the country.

I shall not forget the first of the post-Troubles Horse
Shows which I attended.   The military element had
transformed the Jumping into a major occasion.   All the
Government was there.   The intriguing new Diplomatic
Corps were in force and meeting the Governor-General's
carriage, after it had driven round the ring, were my old
friends the leading " Colonels ", with some impressive
survivors of " Row A ", all of them in their best grey top
hats.

The first of the new short line of King's Representatives
was Mr. Tim Healy, uncle of Kevin O'Higgins, and an
old Parliamentarian.   Whatever his many enemies may
say of him, " Tim " had personality.   His adder tongue
did not impede the coo of the turtle dove.   It was difficult
to believe that this genial and dignified old gentleman had
brought down two so much greater men.   Both Parnell
and Redmond had been winged when his final blows hit
them, but it was his hammer which nailed their coffins,
and for long his venom kept their ghosts stilled.

My husband and I had the good fortune to meet Mr.
Healy personally on the occasion when we were received
by him at Vice-regal Lodge.   To risk more metaphors :
our host then united the charms of devilled almonds,

crême de menthe and Pêche Melba, perfectly blended. He
clearly enjoyed the turn of the wheel which had once laid
him on the plank prison bed but now connected him with

MY OLD FRIENDS THE LEADING " COLONELS," WITH SOME IMPRESSIVE
SURVIVORS OF " ROW A."

the Crown. He told us he was sending His Majesty a Dainty Dish as Christmas present ; twenty-four woodcock baked in a pie.

He led us to the French window giving a winter's view across the Phoenix Park. " Yes ", he said pensively, " I often think I would make a tempting target standing here." Times were still disturbingly uneasy and I must have moved back an inch. " Don't be afraid ", he protested. " You see I keep all my best Waterford glass in the same line of fire " ; he showed us the cabinet on the back wall where his treasures rested and held up a conserve jar to catch the light. The defiance of leaving what he loved best where he did was part of his audacious confidence that made his enmity so dangerous. His nephew, Kevin O'Higgins, was a far finer man but he had inherited the family hammer and he could drive a tin-tack out of sight. It was the same audacity that took him unarmed and alone to Mass on that fatal Sunday morning. Had it been Tim, one feels he would have placed avengers near at hand.

Interest in O'Higgins did not die with him. It is admitted how much his outlook affected the flexibility of the Commonwealth. His grasp of essentials is still talked of by those who study the framing of the Statute of Westminster. His friends naturally incline to quote his views to support their own special bias, whilst his detractors suggest that the subsequent failing of these friends derived from the example given them by their leader. General O'Duffy, his special colleague and appointed by him to be head of the Civic Guard, became tainted with Fascism, and through him the memory of O'Higgins suffered. It is left an open issue, but his admirers deny that he would have succumbed to the tendency.

When Ragnar Östberg, the Swedish architect, visited
Dublin, I sat next to O'Higgins at a long luncheon
given by Trinity College.   He had a reticent manner but
his sense of authority was outstanding.   He could see
ahead and I believe his loss to the country can still be felt.
Impressed by the fine surroundings of the College, he was
all the time looking around him and repeated, " This is
what the young ought to have ; dignity and tradition."
Although the hardest hitter, O'Higgins was not a man of
war, nor, curiously enough, with few exceptions, were the
majority of the leaders whom I knew.   General Mulcahy,
who had gained the fiercest reputation of them all, was
the kindest and most humane among them.   What a life
he and his family led during those years !   No man had
as many pledged enemies waiting to kill if they could.
The day I had tea with him and his wife there were six
armed detectives hidden in the garden, watching every

HORSE RACING WAS NEVER SO POPULAR

move. I found my appetite was very shaky. The effect
of the suspense and the occasional shock during that period
of broken peace may have been trifling compared with
full war but it was destructive of social confidence ; it
was so baffling and so near.

Everyone sought to recover the normal. Horse racing
was never so popular, the Dogs had begun ; " Talkies "
were born and games flourished. Rugby and Association
might have suffered under the Gaelic " ban ", which prohibited any player of the Gaelic games (principally their
special football and hurling) even from looking on at a
" foreign " game. The big Roman Catholic colleges,
however, paid no attention, nor did the National
University Colleges of Dublin, Cork and Galway.
Gradually the effect of the ban wore too thin to signify,
but, even now, it has not been abolished ! It seems strange
to stress the influence of games in a chapter headed as
grimly as this one, and yet how vitally they reflect the
interests of normal youth.

From 1916 to 1924 young Irishmen had ceased to play
games ; every energy was focussed on the Cause. Nothing
more reveals the difference between regular and irregular
warfare. In a regular army a drummer boy is only too
ready to go off and kick a football ; in the irregulars the
same lad, bored by games, would crouch in a ditch to look
after his hidden rifle and his ammunition store. Seven
years of unnatural youth were now replaced by the fun
of normal recreation. Perhaps the ban helped some of
the more patriotic to feel they were still on service when
they turned their back on " treasonable " matches. Stray
shots would still ring out, threats appear, until intimidated
juries were superseded by military courts. These continued during Mr. de Valera's government. One hesi-
tates to mention the date of the " final ' shooting lest it

should come to belie its name. The burst of violence which crossed over to England met with such condign punishment there that it did not endure for long.

In the struggle to restore order the Cosgrave Government was well served by its Judiciary ; the Bench, comprising many of its original members, maintained the admirable impartiality of the old *régime,* one of the best heritages which we owe to Britain and the happiest tribute to this " Sweete Civilitie " of Spencer. Our judges have been well chosen and well paid and the new system of District Justices (drawn from the Solicitors' Roll) has succeeded the amateur J.P.s and the former Resident Magistrates.

The Civic Guard, replacing the R.I.C., was the creation of O'Higgins who took the risk of leaving the force unarmed except for a truncheon. To the old Unionists nothing has been more unexpected than the standard achieved by these young men under their own officer class. We had been brought up to accept the axiom that, unless led by their superiors, i.e. by us, no Irish police force could be trusted. The R.I.C. was our ideal example of leader and led, with the choicest often translated into the Irish Guards. Undoubtedly there have been misfits in the new force and some bad batches got in ; yet, after about thirty years, sometimes of great trial, the Garda is respected and trusted by the public and feared by the law-breaker. In many small ways they have shown tact as well as firmness. They undertook the Civil Service duties involved by rations, permits and customs with patience and understanding. In contrast with the native Irish, the ex-British have taken an important lead in the protection of animals. R. Martin of Galway was the originator of the Society for the Prevention of Cruelty to Animals.

The small Irish Army has also maintained its political independence. During the Second War it became larger and better armed and some of the old Army N.C.O.s joined and were used in their old ranks. Except in the technical branches, the officers are chiefly drawn from the better educated farmer class. It certainly appeared sad and wasteful that so much of the training of the old Irish regiments could not be revived and used, but in the early days of the new Army difficulties would have been great. During the Second War many Protestants enlisted but, as our neutrality became stiffer, most of them left for more active fields. In peacetime, the Anglo-Irish officer class, however well intentioned, could hardly have fitted in with the new. No division made by man is as unbridgeable as class and, instead of unity, it is likely that only ill-feeling would have been evoked, especially on the social side, where the wives would also have been implicated. The Anglo-Irish vividly remembered the Mecca of the pre-war Curragh and the smart old days. Unfair and unkind comparisons would have been made.

While the new Irish Army was slowly taking shape it received little encouragement from Unionist circles. Indeed the popular anecdotes that went the rounds did no credit to the tellers. Regular Army men, when they encountered the new units, were more understanding ; they noted the well cleaned leather gaiters and belts of the officers, the smart marching of all ranks, and the captive gloves under the privates' shoulder-straps. The staging at the Horse Show was a telling shop window, even if the Ruritanian Hussar uniforms lacked the conviction of traditional corps. The Dublin Fusiliers are no longer with us, but many of their sons may be serving in old barracks and their forebears would not be ashamed to acknowledge them now.

CHAPTER XIV

HARP RESURGENT.

With the establishment of the Free State Government and the formation of our own civil frame work, the Harp was polished up and regilded. True, an important string was missing, which prevented the harmony of a single national air. Officially a minute crown remained on the top, but it was not rivetted in consent and its hold was precarious. Sometimes one questions whether the choice of this beautiful and romantic instrument as our national emblem has been happy ; according to my dictionary, the verb " to harp " is taken from the instrument and means " to dwell tediously ". Can we deny this failing ? The Laments for the Sorrows of Erin have reduced that dignified figure from the Queen she should be almost to Pauper. Erin would make a splendid model for the obverse of a coin if we only allowed her to sit up straight.

In this connection, where the Crown remains without demur is in our pockets. British money circulates here and Britannia (bolt upright) still queens it on the half-penny. Even since the issue of our own handsome coinage, English currency runs in Eire in concord with ours. At the time of the new issue, the then Minister for Finance told me that the suggestion of showing two sparrows on our farthing had been considered but the woodcock was found more decorative. This special form of anchorage to the £ was often criticised but several expert committees supported it, and during our early days we probably derived as much stability from this constant as the shaky world of credit affords. To have " the dear King's head " in our handbags was, and still is, a redeeming solace to many nice old ladies.

It was not until 1925 that my husband decided to move his office from England to Dublin. His work as Deputy

MY MOTHER WAS EAGER TO RETURN TO THE DUBLIN SHE HAD
KNOWN IN HER YOUTH

Chief Architect of the Housing Department had ended and he was now on his own. It shows the acceptances at the time of our marriage that a man practising in London was likely to get better jobs in this country than if he operated solely in Ireland. Proof of this is to be seen in the huge works executed in Dublin by Sir Aston Webb and other Englishmen.

My father had died in 1923 and my mother was eager to return to the Dublin she had known in her youth and which she longed to see in its changed guise. We all decided to come over and set up shop together.

At that time many more people were shaking the dust

of Ireland off their feet than coming in. When our three Pickfords arrived at Raglan Road windows flew up and Colonels' and old ladies' heads popped out to see the strange sight. It almost affected the property market that anyone *for no reason* should come to live in Dublin. None of us regretted the adventure, least of all my mother ; she loved entertaining and in the six years before she died made many new friends. At her parties she delighted to see the " Turtle lying down with the Alderman " and in mixing her ingredients. She combined two loyalties not often found together, an unshaken attachment to the wearers of the Crown, which did not contradict an intense love for Ireland. As the widow of a general in the British Army, she was a sad disappointment to some of her Dublin callers. I remember the somewhat ruffled departure of one such, topped by what my mother called a Rule Britannia hat, who had been deploring the lamentable contrast between present days and the lovely old times which my mother must have remembered at the Castle. The reponse was hardly what she expected. When she left my mother watched her walk down the granite steps and remarked " and the poor woman had not even got the profile for the tumbrils."

My mother had the keenest admiration for Mr. Cosgrave and his party and I doubt that she would have adjusted herself to the change of government that came so soon after her death in 1931.

My husband, on the contrary, was without partisan feeling. Erskine Childers, the elder son of the author, told me that he had never even heard of an Irishman so little interested in party politics. He was ready to place his experience where it was needed and asked for and was more concerned to co-operate in getting the things he valued done than in their political or patriotic com-

plexion. At that time there was a movement to remove
the supposed nationally offensive sight of Nelson's Pillar
from O'Connell Street. My husband with other competent critics considered this to be the finest column in
Europe (I note that Dr. Bodkin's plea for the creation of
an Irish Fine Arts Commission is based on the need to
prevent such a type of iconoclasm) and at once took up
its defence, declaring that he was quite uninterested in
the personality of whoever was at the top. This, of
course, shocked the ex-Unionists. The only other
citizens who saw the problem with his detachment were
the old women selling bananas round its base. They
valued the slowing down of the traffic by their pitch.
Thirty-five years have passed since then but Nelson and
Parnell, the two defiant lovers, remain within easy hail
of each other in O'Connell Street, witnesses to the
complications of men's hearts.

The Irish have no personal animosity to the sailor ;
true, individuals were liable to be handed over to the
naval press gang under the Irish Insurrection Act of 1796,
which made *untried* seditious suspects eligible for seizure.
Grattan and the Lawrence Parsons of his day had both
hotly opposed the measure. When their service was over
such sailors, like Wellington's soldiers, received no pen-
sion but were allowed the privilege, if in acute distress,
of begging publicly without arrest.

Dublin, as a capital city, has a unique distinction.
Nowhere else would a visitor, dropped from the skies, at
once know where he was. If we leave out of account the
half-dozen shopping and office centres, which resemble
their counterparts the world over, the impress of Dublin
is single and complete. Our visitor would find himself in
a broad street or generous terrace, flanked by sober red-
brick houses. There would be granite details, vast flights

of steps, and well-proportioned doors crowned with fan-lights ; the skyline of the roofs might be interrupted with a disregard of general unity but, whether the street dated from 1750 or 1850, the family likeness would be un-mistakable — Dublin. The main material is its own, the red brick from the clay on the site. The houses around Merrion Square overlook the hollow from which, accord-ing to tradition, the clay for the bricks was extracted. The granite comes from beyond the city boundaries, and its use with and alongside the brick typifies that union of street and mountain, which is so distinctive of the city.

If there were no other justification for the Anglo-Irish occupation even the most vindictive Nationalist, if he had any taste, would have to concede us 18th century Dublin.

There it stands with all its magnificence in front and despite decaying squalor behind, a capital city, built for gentlemen, designed by artists and fashioned by ingenious Irish craftsmen. It was the seat of our first Parliament that showed spirit and how superbly we housed it ! It was the magnet for the " sperritted " Volunteers when Charlemont and Kildare headed their demonstration. It was the same Lord Charlemont who left us the house now used for our picture gallery to welcome the Lane Collection and who also erected that exquisite conceit, the " Casino ".

Because of the architectural legacy which we have in-herited, we are able to house our present Parliament, Customs, Bank and State Offices in monumental settings. When we receive distinguished visitors they are enter-tained in Iveagh House in an atmosphere of quality. Moreover, there is the spacious lay-out, when left un-disturbed and as the designers planned it.

Perhaps it was because literary Dublin had been favourably disposed towards my husband's writings, that we were lucky enough to receive the freedom of that city's most pleasant social circle. It is interesting to look back on that curious period of interlude ; although actually so formative, to those living in it at the time it appeared as an undirected *cul de sac*. People had become numbed by events and cynicism was general. The enthusiasm of the young men in the Government was not backed by public optimism. They were not well known and their administrative ability was untried. It is understandable that they should have adventured early on the big project of the Shannon Electric Scheme. People needed something on the grand scale to occupy their minds and, even if it might have been less costly had it followed and not preceded the cement factories, it did much to widen horizons when we were too prone to look inwards. Criticism of the measure was chiefly focused on the unlikelihood of " the backward Irish " becoming electrically-minded and of using up the amount of power to be provided.

To Anglo-Irishmen, who were used to the country only, the mental climate of Dublin was unexpected. It was exciting to discover that so many of our own kith and kin had been on the Irish side in the conflict. Much of this trend had been due to indignation over the arming of Ulster, strengthened by disapproval of the methods used after the 1916 outbreak. That affair and the destruction it involved had been generally unpopular in Dublin, but the tactless handling of the executions, more than their extent, caused opinion to swing round and, by 1920, with the Black-and-Tans to add fuel to the disapproval, the national resistance had spread to many Protestant quarters. To meet educated people of our own social outlook, holding these views, was new and provocative. The hyphenated Irish are so much associated with country

reactionaries that it is essential to stress the contribution
which these others have paid to significant Irish life.

Social tolerance was, however, extremely broad, although, until Mr. de Valera's party came into power, the
Republican element was less ready to mix with those
supporting the Free State.

Among the influences in Dublin none was more marked
than that of the distinguished old lady, Miss Sarah
Purser. Nationalist in sympathy, she came of a family
of scholars, all of them Moravians in faith, and she lived
in a country house surrounded by its own demense in
which cows browsed, a mile from the centre of Dublin.
Mespil House was early Georgian and Miss Purser had
secured portraits of the previous owners in order that she
might recognise their ghosts. When young she had been
a successful portrait painter in constant touch with French
artists, but her best-known activity was the stained-glass
industry she had founded and then run co-operatively
with the crafts workers. One of these designed the new
window at Eton.

Her " Second Tuesdays "— every month — were after-
noons reserved by her friends for Mespil House. Here,
helped by her brother, Dr. Louis Claude Purser, F.T.C.D.,
she received her intimates and everyone active in Dublin
life. We were not *all* expected *every* Tuesday and it required subtlety of discernment to know whether one
might be scolded for having missed too many of the
fixtures, or receive a slightly " What, you again ? " on a
crowded day. Miss Purser's tongue, using the old
fashioned brogue of her generation which was educated
in Ireland, could be sharp ; nothing could more keenly
stab through the bogus. Her kindness was unfathomable
and was shown by the cohort of very dull and dowdy
friends who were welcomed, indeed expected, *every*

Second Tuesday. I often wondered what happened to this pathetic brigade after that final date — a " Second Tuesday " it was too — when we all met at her funeral. She had lived every minute of her over ninety years, and during the last ten exercised a welding but imaginative influence at a most critical time. Her achievement was such that afterwards no one else attempted to carry it on.

Her practical memorial to the young, in whom she was so much interested, remains in the substantial scholarship for the study of Historical Art she gave, in conjunction with her cousin, Sir John Purser Griffiths (the originator of the Poulaphouca Hydro-Electric Scheme). This is awarded in alternate years by T.C.D. and the National University and I am proud that my daughter, Olivia, should have gained it in 1943.

Nobody else had an " Afternoon " but there were many " drop-in-for-coffee " evenings. The first of these which we attended was the Con Currans' Wednesday. Con was the principal Registrar at the High Court, where he was reputed to know as much of law as he did outside it of Georgian craft work. His wife I shall claim as Scotto-Irish, although she was better known as a Roman Catholic Nationalist. She had been a player in the original Irish Theatre movement before it went to the Abbey and she told of the night she had played Cathleen Ni Houlihan when George Wyndham, Chief Secretary, brought a party of earnest young English officials to the theatre. She determined to put every word through his soul and Wyndham, most sensitive of beings, was obviously shattered by the experience !

Of all the parties " Con's " was the most varied. I remember the time I met Sean Lester, afterwards High Commissioner for the League of Nations at Danzig. He was much excited when I confessed that I had been a

Unionist and he declared (which was, of course, untrue) that he had never met one.   He drew his chair nearer : " Now you will explain to me what it feels like to be a Unionist and I will tell you what it's like to be on the run."   We had a lovely evening ; the most memorable part was the account he gave of O'Higgins' genius of personality.   This was a week before the tragedy.   After it I wrote to him and said what I could.   I have kept his reply because it shows the type of mind which was drawn to a movement we had at one time thought consisted of unlettered gunmen.   We must surely acknowledge that these men who collected the loose stones from amongst the rubble of destruction and built the foundations of the state did not do so badly.   It was not until many years afterwards when reading of his death I learnt that Lester was Protestant Anglo-Irish to add to our rota of successes, on a European standing.

It was at the Currans' that we met AE and became frequent visitors to his Sunday evenings.   There, perched on various, most uncomfortable chairs and boxes, we ate slab cherry cake, cut by the unobtrusive Mrs. AE in the background.   Seated like a sage and Buddha, AE would boom away with equal interest to any of us.   It might be to James Stephens or the T.C.D. Professors Bergin and Edward Curtis the historians ; or to George O'Brien, economist of the National, or to Frank O'Connor.   One evening it was to A. L. Rowse, who answered back in an impeccable Oxford intonation.   He found Dublin very reactionary.   The walls were hung with mystic figures seen during the days when AE used to see such things. He admitted that he had since lost faith in short cuts to the Beyond because, he declared, the images and messages were so often misleading and spiritually were undepend-able.   By the institutionally minded he was called agnostic ; actually there was no more religious man and he loved people to go to Church. His work with Sir Horace Plunkett in the cause of co-operation meant as much to him as his higher mystic flights, proving that the practical and the profound are complementary at the highest levels ; perhaps the same.

He knew the most intimate details of farming finance and I heard him depress a chicken enthusiast by declaring that the only man he knew who made anything out of poultry was one who took in pupils. At that time he edited the *Irish Statesman*, our Parish Pump of everything interesting in Ireland. Its columns welcomed both ideas and information, sometimes from the strangest newcomers, and its collapse, after an unfortunate libel action, was a disaster ; it had, however, given strings to the Resurgent Harp when its voice was muted and had helped to make it a better instrument. Shortly after the failure AE left Dublin and, before we realised he had decided to stay away for good, he died.

As the Diplomatic elements developed, entertaining became more formal, but many of the intimate " evenings " continued even during the War. It was then that one might meet Eleanor, now Lady Wicklow, (née Eleanor Butler, the young architect), discussing Francis Johnson with John Betjeman, sometime Press Attaché for Britain. No member of the " C.D." in Dublin ever made so many friends as did John. He loved unearthing the Illustrious Obscure and the architect Johnson was an ideal quest. Eleanor's friends have not yet decided where her many outstanding gifts are going to lead her.

Most of the personalities I have mentioned happened to be Anglo-Irish. To claim that they all were would be to flog a living horse and neglect their special contribution to the mixture of our social life.

The cynicism of the first years in Dublin was gradually replaced by more confidence in ourselves. Largely due to Proportional Representation, our first Government lasted ten years and our second twenty, restoring our belief in stability. Moreover public and local administration was more efficient and straighter than we had dared to hope. Mr. T. P. O'Connor had told me there was nothing the Irish Parliamentary Party more feared than petty venality and favouritism in local affairs. The Sinn Fein people declared disparagingly that this danger would have been greater with the old Parliamentarians, whose supporters expected much butter on their paws. Anyhow, Mr. Cosgrave took no chances and instituted a machinery for appointments which Mr. de Valera continued, both of them in the teeth of hot local opposition. No permanent public appointment carrying a minimum salary can be made except on the recommendation of the Appointments Commissioners. These are outside personalities, with an impartial Chairman, who are selected afresh to recommend the Minister on each appointment. If they have made mistakes, they have seldom been influenced by graft or favouritism and their example is beginning, ever so slightly, to form a more responsible public opinion. With the entry of the Fianna Fail Party into the Dail, the hard barrier between the two sides softened slightly, and those outside the ring met the Republican Party socially, but it was not until the Republicans attained power that the Crown connection began to crumble. The successor to Mr. Tim Healy had also been appointed by the Cosgrave Government. Mr. James MacNeill, who had been a high official in the Indian Civil Service, was a member of a cultivated, scholarly family; he had dignity and experience and he maintained the status of Personal Representative which was contained in the

Constitution. His wife, equally cultivated and a brilliant musician, had had a career of contradictory experiences. She had been Mr. de Valera's Secretary during the Civil War. Later in London, as a friend of the Laverys, she met MacNeill and, influenced by him, did what only a strong-minded woman could do, she changed her political opinion. After their marriage he accepted the appointment of Governor General and his wife carried off her role regardless of outside criticism. After his death, as Minister for Eire in the Netherlands, for many years she represented her country with innate distinction.

When Mr. de Valera, after his accession to power, decided to change the status of the Crown, MacNeill's position was made impossible and he retired. His successor agreed with Mr. de Valera to treat the post as of no account and merely held the line until the Constitution was changed and a President appointed.

The choice of that popular Anglo-Celt, Douglas Hyde, as the first President was a masterpiece. Here was someone whom everybody liked and respected;; a Protestant who preferred to speak Irish ; a scholar and poet, a country gentleman who was an excellent shot at snipe, and a democrat. What a gift from the Gods ! It almost placated those who mourned the loss of a Personal Representative. As he was an old connection of my mother's Graves' cousins we had known him well since our first arrival in Dublin. The "Arus", as the Viceregal Lodge was now named, became a home from home to most of Ireland, or rather of Eire, as the Constitution had dubbed us.

It was certainly not Mr. de Valera's intention to coin a neat name, easily spelt and of faintly Gaelic flavour, to distinguish the larger part of separated Ireland. To him Eire means the thirty-two counties. To everyone else it means twenty-six, a most convenient, if unpredicted, asset for Partition.

The early years of the Fianna Fail Government were marked by the Economic War, the last phase of the Land Acts. Hitherto the occupying tenants paid the annuities for the purchases of their holdings to the Land Commission, who passed it on as interest on the capital advanced by England. Mr. de Valera was advised that, owing to a legal flaw in the Treaty conditions, this annual payment was not due to England but to the Irish Government. The British lawyers did not agree and sanctions were applied by both sides.

The struggle, with the consequent slaughter of calves and drastic reduction of stock, ran a bitter course. In the final settlement the Annuities were allotted to Eire in return for a moderate (token) cash sum whilst Irish sensibilities were met by the British ceasing to occupy our ports, at that time not regarded as of prime account, or as urgent as was improved good-will.

After Dr. Hyde's retirement he was succeeded by Mr. Sean T. O'Kelly, a member of the Government. This was resented as a political choice, although it is more likely that an agreed candidate had not fancied the post. No one could have complained of Mr. O'Kelly's energy and impartiality and his wife, a qualified analytical chemist, was equally active in public work.

Owing to air transport Dublin is now visited by a string of international celebrities. The increased status of the Diplomatic Embassies adds to official fixtures. The intimacy of the Twenties has given way to full dress functions and a new formality.

CHAPTER XV

CROWN DIMINISHED.

Those evenings of the Thirties in Dublin were opportunities for good talk, free and uninhibited — no, perhaps
not uninhibited, there were some things about which you
would be apprehensive — differences were only delightful
when they did not touch the quick of the nail. Those in
authority at Radio Eireann told Manning that it was
impossible to keep up a wide range of Radio discussion in
Dublin because so few differences of opinion will be expressed aloud. The same people who will hurl personal
abuse at those they think have wronged or slighted them
will yet adhere to taped judgments and avoid the slightest
taint of criticism. It is at this point that the Anglo-
element might stiffen us but, even there, those who should
be bold enough to take the lead are unlikely to go to the
microphone and say in public discussion what they really
feel.

Among the burning topics of those years Compulsory
Irish was an easy first. This, it must be explained, was
not the Gaelic of the League and the Literary Twilight,
which some considered the mere hobby of the cultured
and romantic. Some of the most prominent among these
scholars were less acceptable than the completely ignorant
because they openly admitted that they disliked compulsion. The young men who had just laid down their
swords believed with fervour that only the whole hog
could unite the country to become distinctively Irish
again. It was essential, they claimed, to recover the
national hall-mark which the British had deliberately

167

taken from us, nothing else would allow us to step forth in nation-hood. Therefore anyone who opposed this purely political ideal was " West British ". Some of the most responsible scholars refused to wear the gold *fainne* of Irish speakers and were regarded as the worst deserters. Yet those who disliked compulsion rarely did so for " West British " reasons, since political opposition was the one thing which might have made the decision effective. I never met anyone opposed to the voluntary mastery of Gaelic. Both of our sons attained moderate efficiency and it is interesting now to remember that it was Douglas Hyde himself who told me that he regarded thirteen as the most useful age to start learning a second language. Our two sons began Irish only when at that age they went to St. Columba's. However, the country was obviously entitled to keep up the language if it so decided and most of us assented without enthusiasm to majority pressure. Compulsion was pursued with fanatical conviction.

Now, after a full generation's experiment, the Irish Language is only heard in the homes of some teachers, instructors and civil servants, who are native speakers. Most of us believe that a wholly voluntary approach, after primary school years, would have shown better results. It could hardly have had feebler ones. Yet to this day people are shy of saying what they really think and of becoming unpopular or of being thought " West British "; this phobia has spread to many other topics which grown up people are entitled to discuss if they wish. We Anglo-Irish have so much helped to reveal the glories of the Gaelic story, and have so many enthusiastic volunteers among us, that we are fully entitled to express our attitude towards compulsion without being vilified. There is still, unfortunately, an under-current of dislike against " West Britons " throughout the country, mostly fostered by white collared desk people. Those working on the land or in industry are uninterested, indeed friendly. To meet this " Fee-foo-fum " complex by nervous silence is futile. Let us say what we feel without being unnecessarily provocative.

Alas ! how apt poor Campion's indictment still appears :

" Greedy of prayse they be and fearful of dishonour." Dishonour including any critical slant on country, religion, or morals, even if the slant is not wholly adverse.

Beyond the din of compulsion, the inspiration of the Celtic tradition and language remain, but more for individuals than for a group. Scholars find continued nourishment in its texts but its initial impetus has lost drive. As it stands, the achievement has brought a quality to our literature, setting it apart from any other of its time, even its Scottish cousin. The myths on which it is founded, with their recurrent echoes and constant movement, lack the ice hardness and outline of Grettir and Gisli, or the intellectual and worldly background of the Greeks. The appeal woos us from a queer uncertain region. If Yeats passed on from the Gaelic world, his sojourn there affected his last immortal period of the " Vision " and the apex of his achievement.

James Stephens, whom we often met at AE's, was also attacked on patriotic grounds and he too was affected by the myth in every word he wrote even when it did not directly appear. Lord Dunsany coquetted with, but did not achieve, the Celtic ideal and his best work remains independent of it.

It is tempting to suggest that the group is still unified by the quality, differently experienced, that has run through it, even from Spenser's day. The sense of comparison and query — what we have called paradox —

seems always present, appraising, but more often contend-
ing, making it selfconscious, yet keenly aware. During
the deepest immersion in the Celtic mood this quality was
overlaid, but not for long. It became keener in James
Stephens and Synge, but only when profoundly lived as
by Douglas Hyde and AE did the Gael overcome the
hyphen. In Protestant O'Casey, who chose the slums,
the paradox is startling and his frustration over here was
a dramatic calamity.

During his last years, when he was becoming too old to
be dangerous to us, we began to preen ourselves in the
light reflected upon us by the world glamour of Shaw.
Yet can there be any other people so much out of touch
with everything he stood for ? Shaw the Fabian, fascinated by reform, whether municipal, dietary, or alphabet-
ical ! His thrusts at marriage, hell, drink, smoking,
vivisection, Chocolate Soldiers, Little Black Girls and
Mrs. Warren make us cringe. It is in fact astonishing
that amongst us only the Wexford Bee Keepers' Society
should have drummed him from their midst. Perhaps
his innate asceticism reassured us or his constant claim to
be Irish flattered us. Anyhow we all regretted that he
could not be buried alongside the Dean in St. Patrick's
Cathedral. What a funeral we should have given him !
It would have been an epilogue in Tall Hats, and Shaw
loved epilogues.

Among the Literary World Yeats was the celebrity we
personally knew best. As fellow Savile Club members
in London, he and Manning had been acquainted and he
was the kindest senior to him from the time we came to
live in Dublin. He was then a Senator and he gave much
time to his duties, especially devoting himself to education
in its humdrum details. He took a personal pride in the
new Government's administrative success and their zeal

to obtain a good Army band, under "that German *Brasso* " ! (Colonel Brasse).

One night when he was dining with us he was particularly interested in the observations of Joseph O'Neill, then Secretary to the Department of Education. O'Neill, a native Gael, had been reared an Irish speaker but had rapidly shot ahead in the academic world. That evening Yeats queried the influence of the English public schools and asked O'Neill directly for his views. O'Neill evidently wished to express a considered opinion but he clearly surprised W.B. by his reply : " The public schools have given England her eminence in the world — ah ! but not as they think : they have taught Englishmen a subtlety of contact between man and man. That is their special art." I sometimes wonder whether this tribute influenced Yeats in his decision to send his son, Michael, to one. He was with our boys at St. Columba's.

It would be impertinent for me to mention more than the trivia which I personally knew of Yeats ; but then keen interest in the simplest things was a part of his nature. I can see him, sitting with his long stick held between his knees, watching every stroke in a boys' cricket match. He could hardly be led away to tea from the exciting field.

He loved detective stories and if he found me at the R.D.S. Library, he would call me over to help to choose *the best* for him. He was conspicuously a family man and delighted in his brother Jack's paintings, leading the opinion which inclines to place the two on the same plane of genius. Jack and one of their sisters had that natural clairvoyance which W.B. told us he envied and longed for. He was aggrieved that such a gift, together with musical appreciation, had been denied to him. I have heard him and AE, when they knew no musician was present, blithely decide that *rhythm*, which they could understand, was much the most important quality in music.

I had the good fortune to be present at the office of the film censor the day W.B. witnessed his first film. After it ended he got up ceremoniously and addressed us : " I have been introduced to a new entertainment value ! " (AE said much the same when I was his escort on his first visit to Woolworths !) I do not know why it should have been my good fortune to accompany these men on such paltry occasions but I always regret that I could not follow up W.B.'s pressing invitation, almost a command, to visit them at their new Dundrum home and teach him to play croquet *properly*. He and Mrs. Yeats entertained most hospitably in their large house in Merrion Square. The drawing room often would be lighted by only a pair of high candles, standing wake-like on an oblong table.

Once when introduced into this dramatic setting my husband, tired by a long day's work, was told to sit down. " Now ", said W.B., " I will read you ' Deirdre of the Sorrows ' ". He boomed the verse, listening to and savouring every nuance of his words. But the room was over-heated and the light was dim and the sound was so deep and even that Manning found himself lying on it . . . . asleep.

My husband was a guest on the occasion when the Oliver Gogartys had a party to meet Sir Edwin Lutyens, in whose office their son was working. Lutyens had also been a pupil of Sir Ernest George and as soon as my husband, a reserved man and fellow pupil, came in he cried out : " a brother architect ! " and kissed him on both cheeks. That day Sir Edwin was in irrepressible, puckish form and his eye lit up when Yeats made his dignified entrance and was, with much solemnity, presented by Mrs. Gogarty. With heavy courtesy Yeats began : " And for how long, Sir Edwin, do you propose — ? " " I don't propose. I'm always accepted ", said Lutyens, giving a little dance. Yeats gazed at him. Somebody mentioned Shaw. " Ah ! to be shore ! " capped Lutyens.

After some more of this my husband said he never realised that anyone could look as saddened and puzzled as W.B. Sir Edwin just skipped about like a gleeful school-boy, chose an attractive companion and offered her a lift home in his taxi, waving a gay farewell to the company.

The second War was still being fought when Yeats died in Italy. Mrs. Yeats asked my husband to design his headstone, using the lines he had wished for as inscription. " Cast a Cold Eye on Life and Death. Horseman pass by." For lettering Manning chose the 18th century alphabet taken from " the sperritted Volunteer " in our Clonegal churchyard. The design of the stone followed the " Golden Cut " proportion. After Mrs. Yeats and Jack Yeats had approved it the matter rested until the body could be brought back from Italy to the foot of Benbulben, where it was to lie.

Sometime before this, Mrs. Yeats met my husband and told him that " W.B. liked the stone ". Manning was somewhat taken aback, but I like to think that perhaps W.B. had found on the other side the gift that he had sought for and missed here.

My husband himself did not live to see the impresive funeral given to Yeats by the State, but I know how much he would have been gratified by the choice of the head-stone print as the " still " which ends the official Yeats film.

Our other giant among the writers, Shaw, was not of or in the group of Anglo-Celtic enthusiasts. Blanco Posnet which he offered to Dublin was not an important work. He mentioned, on that day when I met him, the pity it was that the Abbey had not been able to introduce " John Bull's Other Island ". Can anyone believe that it would have escaped a violent reception ? There would have been no Abbey curtain left.

Film censorship in Ireland is a State concern ; in England it is run by the film industry for its own protection. Except in principle few people will fault the attitude of the Irish Film Board in banning films showing horrors, gunmen at work, successful crime, sadism and suicide. Such parades are obviously demoralising to the young and repellent to most people. The argument that, after all, one reads of such events without resentment was wittily countered many years ago by W. S. Gilbert. It was, he suggested harmless to read that " Eliza took off her clothes and stepped into her bath ", whereas the same incident performed on the stage (or screen) might be embarrassing

When the Censorship was first opened in Dublin under its most popular citizen, the late James Montgomery, the tiny theatre where he presided was the *rendezvous* for the elect. He ran off suspect pictures privately and had a formula by which he measured kisses. He would touch his button, stop the picture and ask the operator : " How many feet was that one, William ? . . . .Cut off twenty-five (or whatever it was)". His excision of serious work was always considerate to the author. His well known *mot* that with the film trade on one side and the priests on the other, he was " Between the Devil and the Holy See " reveals his difficulties. Film censorship was almost worth while if only for the consequences which the " terms of reference " produced at our social evenings. As a topic it rivalled Compulsory Irish ; however much the principle does or does not signify, it cannot be denied that the Protestant film-goer attends under a religious umbrella that is not of his choice.

Montgomery, who had been the intimate friend of that moderate and constructive leader Arthur Griffith, was the cream of post-Troubles patriots. Cultivated, shrewd, with a keenly critical mind, he was the seasoning of any gathering. With his coachman's dark stock, his clear complexion and bright eyes, he was as good to look at as he was to talk to. He was deeply devoted to his Church but no man was more broadminded. He told me that his friend and colleague, Canon T. W. E. Drury, the Protestant representative on the Appeal Board, was his stand by, and that he turned to him when in need of impartial judgment.

I walked away from James's funeral with Canon Drury, who had been his constant visitor during his last illness. He said how much and for how long they had been together, and he added that during those years he had watched James grow in grace.

During the Thirties we were chiefly concerned in regaining our normal life and in patching up the breaches caused by the Civil War. Shots were still to be heard in the background, but by the time that the de Valera party had accepted office and joined in our social life, we began to achieve social adolescence. Better roads and motoring linked town with country. Members of the Cosgrave party were now sometimes spoken to by the " Devites " as we called them and the Corps Diplomatique helped to civilise discordancy. We personally knew and liked the Cosgrave party leaders and I recall a tea party with extreme Unionist cousins which I attended with my mother. We were discussing a forthcoming General Election. Our host, a moderate man, said he would vote for Cosgrave. His wife, an intensely bitter woman, who was feeding her pet poodle with morsels of cake as he sat in a chair by her side, remarked viciously " to think that I should have to vote for the murderous pot-boy ! " My mother at once spoke up : " Mr. Cosgrave is a great friend of mine." Another piece of cake was given to and consumed by the poodle to the refrain : " To think that I should have to vote for the murderous pot-boy ! " Never did anyone send up an sos for peace as I did then. To my relief, my mother leant forward :— " What a delightful pug ! " Everyone corrected her and my prayer was answered.

The Devites gradually shook down into social conventions with the rest of us, especially with the Anglo-Irish who had been unconcerned in the Civil War. Life had to go on.

How far the outbreak of the Second World War interrupted or destroyed the solidarity that was beginning to build up between the younger generation of the Irish and the young ex-Unionists it is difficult to say. Most of the latter, inherently attached to the old ideals, could not hesitate. They joined up at once. Because after the firm declaration of neutrality there was no Irish allied army to join, they had to enlist in N. Ireland or England. A few somewhat half-hearted Unionists claimed their undoubted right to neutrality and stayed put. Others undertook work which was not directly concerned with War service in England. There was singularly little criticism of what was felt to be a purely personal decision in a neutral country. That this right to independent judgment was accepted without cavil was remarkable in a community where blue print English loyalty had always prevailed. The enormous response among Roman Catholics as well as Protestants to the appeal of the British Army was astonishing. When the war was over and Censorship permitted Obituary notices to appear in the press whole pages were filled by their names. Indeed it is now known that there was a higher percentage of volunteers from southern Ireland than there had been from Ulster. With no traditional Irish line regiments to join, the Irish Guards, if you were tall enough, or the R.A.F. were the most popular corps.

Admitting this response, the Government neutrality policy is still vehemently resented by Unionists and by the majority of English people. To those of us living here in safety it was a continuous trial and the loss of the Ports to the Navy almost unbearable. To say a word in its possible justification would appear to be special pleading, yet to be fair one must give some of the reasons behind it, especially as I know personally that at least two of the Ministers who were compelled to accept the ruling were themselves entirely anti-Hitler and pro-Ally. When the War broke out the Ports did not signify and the best help Eire could then give the Allies was to grow food and give no trouble. It would be foolish now to deny the amount of definite anti-English feeling which existed in the country, ready to break out on any excuse. This may seem strange in view of the larger pro-Ally support but there it was and its capacity for giving underground trouble was great. Moreover as bombing became more general the civilian population here became increasingly scared. Is this surprising? Did it not take Pearl Harbour to bring in the United States and invasion to involve neutrals? We had received the direct hint that to yield on the Ports meant a devastated Dublin. Were the Ports vital to save defeat? History has shown that they were not. The War was won without them. Far the best statement on the predicament was made by Maj.

General Franks, a distinguished retired gunner. This was embodied in his answer to Northern criticism, both papers being published by the Irish Association (for promoting better relations between North and South). General Franks was one of the many Anglo-Irishmen who could see facts objectively and whose character and opinion were equally respected both here and in London. It is no secret to say now how much Mr. de Valera's Government and the London Cabinet owed to his timing when the economic war was nearing solution. It was he who advised Mr. Malcolm MacDonald as to when to come to Dublin.

Had we come into the War after Dunkirk there was nothing whatever that could have protected us. There was only one fully equipped division in England and she could not then have spared supplies. We should also have been faced by an actively divided country.

The neutrality worked in important ways in Britain's favour. Meteorological reports managed to get direct to Britain but were denied to Germany. The rumour of enemy submarines being helped to refuel on the Kerry coast was hypothetical and never proved. When the War ended there were no British airmen held as prisoners since the excuse had been found that those not on operational flights, as the Germans were, need not be held as p.o.w. Had the Germans in any way crossed our neutrality we all believed that we should have resented it sufficiently to have taken action. Curiously enough — and to their chagrin — there was no strong pro-U.S.A. feeling to contrast with coolness to Britain. The sense of at last being in a position to direct our own destiny seemed to those in power here to be so intoxicating that the use made of it was of less account. Mr. de Valera's unpopular official call at the German embassy to offer sympathy on Hitler's death, was met by a generally welcomed rebuff when the German Minister gravely informed him that he had received no notification that the Führer was dead !

Security censorship went to fantastic lengths of which the high light was the press message from Singapore describing the loss of the " Prince of Wales " as a boating accident.

WELL-TO-DO ENGLISH TYCOONS SEEKING BEEF STEAKS AND BUYING NYLONS.

The general smug feeling of conceit at having preserved our neutrality was emphasised in the extent of the de Valera victory at the next General Election.

The end of the War was followed by a degree of plenty here unknown in England or Europe and ended our complex of inferiority and distress. We were now invaded by well-to-do English tycoons seeking beef steaks and buying nylons. Fear of Moscow attracted people anxious for houses and land, but the return of a Tory Government ended the short boost. We began to discover that our own economic situation was not so rosy, that alone in Europe our farming production still remained what it had been for thirty years. Soon emigration began with a blissful defiance of anti-English propaganda which even an Irishman could not pretend to understand.

CHAPTER XVI

CROWN ERASED.

The constitutional bonds of Commonwealth and Crown under Mr. de Valera were not easy to unravel. Perhaps they were not intended to be ; but at least when his government was in power there was enough Crown concealed in our passports to justify our place as " Commonwealth " in collectors' Postage Stamp Albums. When in 1949 Mr. de Valera's successor, Mr. Costello, believed to be of Comonwealth sympathy, unexpectedly defined our Republic as wholly independent, his ensuing legislation (the External Relations Act) finally unscrewed the Crown from the Harp. Surely the situation was at last made clear ? Not at all ; it was foggier than ever. Apparently even this rupture was more in *posse* than in *esse.* All commercial implications of Commonwealth relations remain as before and in England Irish citizens are not regarded as foreigners ! Like the curse on the Rheims jackdaw, nobody seemed a penny the worse.

Had Unionists in 1922 been told where the next generation was to take them they would have packed up. But the changes came so gradually and were in practice of so little day-to-day account that the final legislation affected neither our Stock Exchange nor the property market. We Southern Protestants accepted the official exchange of the Harp for the Crown because we admitted our minority position and also because the change did not affect our status or personal relations with the Commonwealth.

Whether the future will evolve an entirely new framework carrying its own symbol, which all parties could honour, we do not know. Harp and Crown are unlikely to be surrendered by their partisans and they can no more be stuck together again than could Humpty Dumpty. This handsome design of the Harp crowned will remain a survival of emotional failure, although at the same time geography, economics and the changed human relationship of vast emigration make the two islands more vitally important to each other than the relations between any of the Dominions or Republics which form the Commonwealth.

The end of the War had coincided with what I hope will be the final setting of my personal saga. In 1945 my husband died extremely suddenly in Dublin and I decided to move down to look after his home in Co. Carlow until our son was free to take on the task.

Nothing is more salutary for the late middle aged than to set to and work for their living. I can safely say that in no other way could I have patched up a life that had been wholly dependent on another keenly active personality. With fishing tenants, P.G.s, shrubs, farm, and notably the Irish Countrywomen's Association to make me friends in every class, I feel part of the neighbourhood, instead of being a pensioner, awaiting patiently the assured beautiful funeral with which matriarchs here are rewarded.

I do not propose to conclude with an editorial discourse befitting my years, but I do retain an unshaken confidence that the Anglo-Irish will continue to live here. We believe that even if our hosts sometimes affect to view us with a bilious eye as visitors rather than as the native aborigines they affect to be themselves, they do not desire to turn us out.

We may be too lazy to learn Gaelic, and bored by the

Mystique of Nationality, yet the Land with the enchantment of its hills and the homely smell of its gorse has become our own, just as personally as our shoes are our own.   The people in it are our neighbours and our catechism dins into us that towards them (as we said in the Foreword) we are pledged to do our duty in that state of life into which it has pleased God to call us.

Our Irish neighbours include our Six County friends, and our kinsmen overseas, just as much as the good local Gaels who happily foregather on the great day at Twickenham.

IF WE ARE NOT ALL GAELS, OR PSEUDO GAELS, WE ARE AT LEAST
GOOD AND VERY AUDIBLE IRISHMEN

Listen to the united Irish cheering there !   Can anyone deny that if we are not all Gaels, or pseudo Gaels, we are at least good and very audible Irishmen.